The Many Themes of Nhemamusasa

Fortunate Hove

**Chapters**                                          **Page**

# 1

## Introduction

I am a journalist, missionary, public relations practitioner, and counselor born and raised in Zimbabwe. Shona is my mother tongue. It is one of the major languages spoken in the countryside where I grew up. Living in the country of Zimbabwe exposed me to the rich cultural heritage of the language and customs of the Shona people, which include folktales, music, and dance. I developed a love for oral history because it connected generations as adults told stories of the past in which heroism, love, and legend were the order of the stories. Also encapsulated in the rich storytelling were raw ethnic or gender feelings in the narrations of the characters that represented them. Something which needs to be added to some of the recorded histories. With such a rich countryside influence, I studied Shona as part of my undergraduate studies. Undergraduate studies helped me to understand the structure of the Shona language as we know it.

After graduating from the University of Zimbabwe, I worked on the National Languages Desk of the Zimbabwe Broadcasting Corporation, where I had another opportunity to enhance my translation skills in the language, translating scripts from English to Shona and then presenting them to the vernacular-speaking radio audience. Although I have spent the past twenty years as a missionary in the United States of America, I cherish the desire to strengthen the significance of my mother tongue wherever I am in my interactions with other cultures.

The writing of this book was a spontaneous response to a need by a graduate student at Columbia University. The student is my daughter Shirley Ratidzai Chikukwa, who is studying Ethnomusicology. It was very unusual of her to reach out for help because she has been a very independent researcher and avid reader since she was little. However, when she was presented with Chiwoniso Maraire's rendition of Nhemamusasa, she struggled to find enough written material for her assignment. In frustration, she reached out to me for solace. She had no idea that I had studied Shona in high school and my undergraduate studies. In the process of our discussion, I asked her to text the lyrics to me. Then together, we looked at it critically. The debate yielded enough content to enable her to write thirty-five pages of her paper. To this day, I am unsure if her inability to find adequate resources on her assignment was due to an inability to access available resources or just the absence of enough written content on the popular traditional song Nhemamusasa. I promised her that apart from what we had discussed on the assignment, I would also write a book on the theme, examining the renditions of Chiwoniso and Ambuya Beauler Dyoko. While reviewing the music performed by Chiwoniso could have sufficed for the writing of my book, I felt that adding Dyoko's rendition broadens the issues covered by the song and corroborates some of the arguments on some of the themes highlighted by both pieces.

Although I am more inclined toward the oral history and traditions of the Shona people, I realize that documenting my views on Nhemamusasa shifts my opinions from an informal to a formalized presentation, which enables the book to be used for both academic and personal enrichment from Shona traditions and customs expressed through the song Nhemamusasa.

As I mentioned earlier, had my daughter, who is on an academic pursuit, not brought to my attention the need to write this book, I would not have done so for the simple reason that I may not have been aware of the need to make any such contribution.

## Some of the themes in Nhemamusasa

### 1. An old-world rendition

The song Nhemamusasa belongs to the old world of Shona literature or poetry. As such, it interacts with the historical developments of its time, which only enrich its content if carefully examined. It gives modern Shona society a glimpse into why they were also called VaNyai or Diplomats because of their skill in employing figures of speech to resolve disputes. In listening to Nhemamusasa, one can sense the presence of an atmosphere of tension even if it is not specified- *usaringe zuva nhamo ichauya.* The pressure is something that the community cannot avoid, so life goes on through celebrations of marriage feasts- *prereka mvura mukaranga iwe.*

### 2. *Nhemamusasa is a genre*

Isolating Nhemamusasa as a song without broadening its relationship with the events of the period before the colonization of Zimbabwe takes away from the song's significance. The name of the song and the variations of its presentation distinguish Nhemamusasa as a genre of music that is broad in content, context, application, and meaning. Many aspects of the Shona life are grouped in the Nhemamusasa genre. Shona folklore, linguistics, and history converge in the make-up of the song to make it an authentic Shona piece of music. The mbira and the harmonies blend to evoke many melancholic feelings, laments, euphoria, and celebration in ceremonial events.

3. **Nhemamusasa plays out the Shona belief system of the relationship between the living and the dead.**
   *Tanzwa ngoma kurira*
   *Kana uchitida tinogara pano*

Nhemamusasa converges the spirits of the dead and the living, more so in Ambuya Beauler Dyoko's rendition than in Chiwoniso. There is a conversation between Gwenyambira and spirits- *ndanzwa ngoma kurira, as well as kana uchitida tinogara pano- we hear the sound of the drum. If you receive us, we will stay here.* The souls of the departed know the spiritual law dimension that forbids the dead to mingle with the living except by invitation through rituals that include music playing. This Biblical law is also expressed in Dyoko's rendition of the song. The dead are disembodied, and as such, spirits cannot live with the living except through the medium of a body of a living being or animal. Therefore, in Nhemamusasa, that knowledge by the departed is made evident by their negotiation with Gwenyambira for permission to join the party- *kana uchitida tinogara pano- if you want us, we will stay here* (for the party). The blasting of mbira sound accompanying Nhemamusasa lyrics beckons the spirits of the dead or those in the wild to come to 'the party of the living. This emphasizes the Shona belief that the souls of the deceased have not left their relatives; although physically, their flesh has perished, their spirits never leave the world of the living. However, they await the invitation of the living to cross from their realm to that of the living. Nhemamusasa is a conduit for this interaction, especially in the Dyoko rendition. This has caused many to classify Nhemamusasa as a song for Shona traditional rites, but there are other purposes that the music serves. However, the Shona lifestyle is a blend of the living believing their dead are always around them. Nhemamusasa fulfills this part of the Shona belief system. Still, the element of entertainment that Chiwoniso amply expresses in her rendition applies to the singing of the song at a marriage ceremony- *pereka, pereka, pereka, pereka mvura mukaranga iwe.*

### 4. The escalation of hostilities leading to close combat

Nhemamusasa demonstrates vital tenets of conflict resolution. This is done through a song to expose problems in the community in a bid to settle differences peacefully is what every community aspires for. Still, people will always have differences, and how those problems are addressed can mean the cessation of hostilities or an escalation. Nhemamusasa expresses the presence of conflict-

*roverera museve.* The lament by Ambuya Beauler Dyoko expresses the existence of a marriage dispute, which is described in line with the Shona tradition of complaining through a song.- *kuroora, roora, ndaroora nguruve,*

## 5. Feminist criticism

Gender inequality is expressed in many ways, the chief of which is singing about a woman or women, but there is no opportunity for them to express their opinion. The one blamed for being filthy- *nguruve,* is so labeled, but at no time is her response ever solicited. The woman is talked about but is yet to be heard. What is she saying? We only listen to her voice through Gwenyambira. Whether Gwenyambira represents her actual views is something that the listeners will never know. Gender roles are defined in the song- *pereka, mvura mukaranga iwee* in Chiwoniso rendition. *Hanzvadzi yaamai vako zvaisingarime* also points to a gender role in which a woman is a minor who needs the care of a male relative, which in this case is a brother. Ambuya Beauler Dyoko sings of a husband who laments over a poor marriage- *ndaroora humba-* pig. Roles are defined clearly according to gender- *pereka mvura mukaranga, ndaroora nguruve, hanzvadzi yamai vako zvaisingarime.*

## 6 . Nhemamusasa connects the Continental African and African Diaspora experiences

Working and living in the African American community for about twenty years, I realized a connection between Negro spirituals and some aspects of Nhemamusasa, the chief of which is the relaying of coded messages through song. During the Underground Railroad in the United States, masterminded by Harriet Tubman, spiritual songs were employed to inform slaves about how and when to escape. The themes were coded with religious lyrics, which the enslavers could not decipher, but the enslaved people did. As a result, some slaves decoded the messages correctly and escaped safely. For example, running to safety was coded as crossing the Jordan into the promised land. I stood over the Jordan River.

*I stood on de ribber Jerdon.*

*To see dat ship come sailing ober*

*Stood on de ribber ob Jerdon*

*O, see dat ship sailing by*

*O moaner, donya weep*

*When ya see dat ship come sailin ober*

# History

Nhemamusasa, precedes the advent of
Mfecane in Southern Africa. It was already part of
the Shona folklore and a genre that employed lyrics
that later addressed the effect of Mfecane on some
Shona communities. *Mfecane* refers to a period of
political disruption and population migration in
Southern Africa during the 1820s and 1830s.
Mfecane is a Xhosa word that comes from two
terms, *ukufaca-* means to "become thin from
hunger," and *fetcani*, "starving intruders" It was
Shaka, Zulu, whose organized military with superior
numbers as well as training, which raided other
communities, incorporating many groups into the
Zulu state in South Africa, leading to the escape of
many groups of people who disagreed with Shaka's
leadership style. The disgruntled warriors left
present-day South Africa for other parts of central
and Southern Africa. States like the Ndebele, Gaza,
Swazi, and Ngoni were born due to Mfecane. The
migration due to the disturbance of the southern
African region resulted in some groups moving as
far away as present-day Tanzania, Zambia,
Zimbabwe, and Malawi. The breakaway Zulu army
raided other communities, destroying everything in
their path, employing the scorched-earth policy in
their raids, and destroying their victims' livelihoods.

The lyrics of Nhemamusasa touch on the impact of Mfecane on the Shona people. Maraire and Dyoko allude to life-threatening instability- *wakaringe zuva nhamo ichauya- while you observe the sun, there is impending trouble* (Maraire). Dyoko creates a scene of stabbing *Roverera museve- sinking the arrow (dagga)*, which is an act of piercing a human being at a close range in combat or the slaughter of an animal during hunting. Violence and instability are alluded to in both renditions of the song.

Although Nhemamusasa gives a glimpse into how the average Shona person felt about incessant raids in their communities by newcomers, it is true that in the 1820s onwards, southern Shona people were subjected to attacks from the east, south, and west carried by different groups. Yet it should be borne in mind that although groups from South Africa introduced the practices of raids and abductions, local groups were either drawn into that practice, as they were incorporated into the newcomers' military ranks, or they engaged in such activities on a small scale like the type of marriage called *Musengamombe, in* which a girl was abducted by a man who loved her without her consent, and taken to his home to become his wife. The man would arrange for dowry payment while the woman was at home. This was an acceptable type of marriage among the Shona. The practice did not separate the woman from her family forever. The woman would reconnect with her family after traditional marriage ceremonies were observed and relations strengthened.

There were also miniature Mfecanes within the greater Mfecane, as local groups adopted Nguni-style raids among their neighbors in present-day Zimbabwe. For instance, the Nguni of Ngwana "Masesenyane" and Mpanka passed through Great Zimbabwe and incorporated some Shona before they proceeded north. The incorporated ranks included the Jena of Nyajena- Moyo totem and Lemba of the Zhou totem from the same area. This group came to be known as the Dumbuseya. They engaged in Nguni-style raids in parts of present-day Midlands and Masvingo. The group was defeated by Zwangendaba at Mount Wedza, near Zvishavane. They fled to modern-day Zvishavane, where they continued the Nguni-style raids among the local communities to Belingwe /Mberengwa in Ngowa and Lemba inhabited areas. The Dumbuseya chiefs were Wedza and Mazetese. Life experiences for the average person in this period are summed up in the song Nhemamusasa as Gwenyambira tries to make sense of the changed circumstances in the Shona community. This is not to say that the Shona people were docile victims; the song expresses the need to be vigilant- *ukaringe zuva nhamo cihauya iwee*. The expression in the music is *roverera museve* which sounds like a combat situation.

In the southeastern part of the country, the Gaza Nguni under Manakuza Sotshangane settled in the Sabi/Save area and subjected the Duma to pay tribute. In the southwestern part of Zimbabwe, the Ndebele kingdom was growing through raids and abductions that went as far as the Mashonaland area. For instance, my great-grandmother Sheterai Chihota was abducted from her home in Chihota as a young girl and taken to Matabeleland. Marondera, a town in Mashonaland East, derives its name from *Kuronda- to trek*. People in the areas of Mashonaland, and possibly parts of Manicaland, tried to search for their abducted daughters from the region who had been taken in raids but could not find them.

However, the strength of other raiding groups like the Dumbuseya and local dynasties like the Matsveru House of Chivi presented a challenge to Ndebele expansion and hegemony in the southern parts, which comprise part of present-day Masvingo province. Not all indigenous dynasties and houses were strong enough to resist raids from the different groups emerging south. Some Shona families suffered greatly at the hands of the raiders and abductees, while others waxed strong in their resistance to the newcomers.

## Chapter 2

## Nhemamusasa by Chiwoniso Maraire

*Mhururu!*

*Hiya*

*Hiya ha-a*

*Hoo-horendere hiya*

*Hiya*

*Hiya Ha-a*

*Hoo-horendere hiya*

*Hiya*

*Hiya Hore*

*Hoo- horendere hiya*

*Nhemamusasa*

*Nhemamusasa*

*Wakaringe zuva nhamo ichauya iwe*

*Iwe Nhemamusasa*

*Nhemamusasa*

*Wakaringe zuva nhamo ichauya iwe*

*Pereka, pereka, pereka*

*Pereka, pereka, pereka, pereka, pereka mvura*
*mukarangaiwe*

*Pereka, pereka, pereka, pereka, pereka, mvura*
*mukarangaiwe*

*Iwe Nhemamusasa*

*Nhemamusasa, nhemamusasa, nhemamusasa*

*Nhemamusasa, nhemamusasa, nhemamusasa*

*Mhururu!*

*Haiya, horendere iye-iye*

*Hanzvadzi yamai vako zvaisingarime iwe*

*Haiwa horendende iye-iye iye*

*Hanzvadzi yamai vako zvaisingarime iwe*

*Iye horendende iyewohere ndende*

*Hanzvadzi yamai vako zvaisingarime iwe*

*Haiwa horendende iye-iye- iye*

*Hanzvadzi yamai vako zvaisingarime iwe*

*Iiiiweee!*

*Hoiye iye aha*

*Hoiye iye ehi*

*Hoiye iye aha*

*Hoiye iye ehi*

*Hoiye iye aha*

*Ere iye ehi*

*Hoiye iye aha*

*Hoiye iye ehi*

*Hoiye iye aha*

*Hoiye iye ehi*

*Hoiye iye aha*

*Hoiye iye ehi*

*Hoiye iye aha*

*Ere iye ehi*

*Hoiye iye aha*

*Hoiye iye ehiye*


*Iyere iye*

*Iyere iyerere*

*Iyere*

*Iyere iyerende*


*Mhururu!*


*Werereiye*

*Iye hoiyendende-e*

*Hanzvadzi yamai vako zvaisingarime iwe mukaranga iwe*

 *Awoire-e*

*Werere iye*

*Iye hoiyendende-e*

*Hanzvadzi yamai vako zvaisingarime iwe mukaranga*

 *Awoire-e*

*Werewu, werewu, werewu, werewu*

*Iya hoeyere*

*Hanzvadzi yamai vako zvaisingarime iwe mukaranga*


*Werere iye*

*Iya hoiyendende-e*

*Hanzvadzi yamai vako zvaisingarime iwe mukaranga- iwe*


*Mhururu!*


*Nhemamusasa, Nhemamusasa-a*

*Wakaringe zuva nhamo ichauya iwe mukaranga*

*Awoire-e*

 *Nhemamusasa, nhemamusasa-a*

*Wakaringe zuva nhamo ichauya iwe mukaranga- iwe*

 *Aiya woire*

*Iwe, nhemamusasa, werewu, iye hoyere*

*Wakaringe zuva nhamo ichauya iwe mukaranga*

*Awoire-e*

*Iwe Nhemamusasa, wereu- u*

*Iya  woire-e*

*Wakaringe zuva nhamo ichauya iwe mukaranga- iwe*

*Mhururu!*

## Nhemamusasa by Ambuya Beauler Dyoko

*Roverera museve*

*Hanzvadzi yamai vako zvaisingarime*

*Roverera museve*

*Kuroora roora ndaroora nguruve,*

*Hanzvadzi yamai vako zvaisingarime*

*Hiya woye woyere ona*

*Hanzvadzi yamai vako zvaisingarime*

*Kuroora ndaroora nguruve*

*Hanzvadzi yamai vako zvaisingarime*

*Iya*

23

*woiye*

*worende heya*

*Roverera museve ona*

*Roverera museve*

*Kuroora roora ndaroora nguruve*

*Hanzvadzi yamai vako zvaisingarime*

*Iya*

*Woiye*

*Woyere ndeya*

*Hanzvadzi yamai vako zvaisingarime*

*Kuroora raoora ndaroora humba ini*

*Iye*

*Woye*

*Ha woye a woyere ona*

*Wona*

*Iye woye*

*Ha*

*Woiyere ha*

*Woye wona wauya*

*Hanzvadzi yamai vako zvaisingarime*

Kuroora roora ndaroora nguruve

Hanzvadzi yamai vako zvaisingarime

Iya

Woiyere

Iye worere ndeha

Ha Iye

Aye Ha ayere

Aye Ha ayere

Aye a here

Aye a yere

Aye a yere

Aye a yere

Iye woyere

Aho

Aho ahere

Hona

Iyere woye a

Woiyere a hoye ona

Wauya

Hanzvadzi yamai vako zvaisingarime

*Kuroora roora ndaroora nguruve-e*

*Hanzvadzi yamai vako zvaisingarime*

*Iya Woiyere woyere hona*

*Hanzvadzi yamai vako zvaisingarime*

*Kuroora roora ndaroora nguruve*


*Hani Changamire, Changamire*

*Changamire*

*Changamire*

*Changamire*

*Changamire*

*Tikinya*

*Tikinya*

*Tikinya*

*Tikinya*

*Tikinya*

*Tikinya*

*Tikinya*

*Tikinya*

*Tikinya*

*Tikinya*

*Apo, apo, apo*

*Apo, apo, apo*

*Apo, apo, apo*

*Apo, apo, apo,*

*Apo, apo, apo*

*Apo, apo, apo*

*Hani*

*Ndanzwa ngoma kurira*

*Kana uchitida togara pano*

*Maiwee*

*Ndanzwa ngoma kurira Beauler*

*Kana uchitida togara pano*

*Maiwee*

*Ndanzwa ngoma kurira Cosmas*

*Kana uchitida togara pano*

*Maiwee*

*Tanzwa ngoma kurira*

*Churuwee*

*Kana uchitida togara pano*

*Maiwee*

*Tanzwa ngoma kurira*

*Ayiyere Iye*

*Ayiyere iye*

*Aiyere iyeAyire iye*

*Ayiyere iye*

*Aiyere iye*

*Ayi yere iye*


*Ayiyere iye*

*Ayire iye*

*Kana uchitida togara pano*

*Maiwee*

*Ndanzwa ngoma kurira*

*Kana ucchitida togara pano*

*Maiwe e*

*Hani*

The renditions of the same song by the two artists present contrasting atmospheres. Chiwoniso Maraire's rendition is a celebration during a marriage ceremony with verses punctuated by ululations, while Ambuya Beauler Dyoko gives an atmosphere of conflict. Although the term "marriage ceremony" encapsulates many aspects, ranging from the lobola/ dowry payment to weddings and traditional ceremonies, Chiwoniso's rendition is focused on the tradition in which a bride has joined the new family- a welcoming party. The welcoming of a bride has many activities associated with it, the chief of which is cooking for the family. This is traditionally done the morning after her arrival into the family permanently. Usually, the whole family waits for the bride and her party to serve them breakfast, lunch, and dinner. This is done to give the bride a chance to demonstrate her worth to the new family. The bride helps the family ceremoniously, bathing, feeding, cleaning the yard, and fetching water and firewood. In the song, these rites appear to be performed in an atmosphere where the bride needs encouragement- *pereka, pereka, pereka, pereka mvura mukarangaiwe.* In theessentialat follow, it is important to explore why the bride/*mukaranga* plays center stage in the rendition of the piece by Chiwoniso Maraire.

On the other hand, Ambuya Beauler Dyoko is lamenting in her rendition of the same song, and she points out the issues that are besetting the environment in which she sings her piece of Nhemamusasa. Her atmosphere is tense, and why this is the case is the subject of examination in the following pages.

# Chapter 3

## The unifying nature of Nhemamusasa

In examining the themes of Nhemamusasa, a song that has its foundations in the Shona language and traditions, it is imperative to understand the time the song was sung and the cultural practices in existence at the time, and how those impacted the birth of the music and the meanings associated with the music.

Nhemamusasa dates back to the pre-colonial days of Zimbabwe when Shona society had moved from a hunting and gathering nomadic lifestyle to a sedentary existence with leadership structures and all the forms of that identified ethnic structures, defined mainly by totems. The song coincides with the time of the height of the Nguni invasion and raids in what we know as Mashonaland today. One can argue that Nhemamusasa centers on the woman and her relations with her stimuli. The song slices a section of the Shona society, the woman or girl child, and explores the dynamics around her in the music. Although not much is documented about the experience of the internal forced migration of Shona women from parts of Mashonaland to Bulawayo or to any community that engaged in raids, except through oral transmission, it is clear that internal enslavement of sections of society was exercised by those who were more robust through the payment of tribute. Women were essential in sustaining peace among tribes through arranged marriage ties. Men also were valuable in replenishing the ranks of raiding groups with ties with armies moving northward, fleeing the terror of Shaka.

This writing is not intended to foment dissension but to explain the artistic sophistication of the Shona Gwenyambira in articulating the vices prevailing in their environment through the song Nhemamusasa. This, of course, is said with the complete understanding that Chiwoniso and Ambuya Beauler Dyoko are not the songwriters of the piece they performed, though they do justice to the song in performance. The critiquing of the rendition comes from an appreciation that songs like Nhemamusasa, with their undertones of pain, remind the people of Zimbabwe that they are related by blood. However, some are called Shona, others Ndebele, Shangaan, and the like. Shona women built the Ndebele kingdom in Zimbabwe, and there is no way that their children can claim to be unrelated to the Shona people. This demystifies the obsession with ethnic exclusivity from both sides because blood ties are robust.

To this author, Nhemamusasa is a foundational song that tells us not to frown at each other because we are one people, but the oneness comes through much pain. It is a painful past that should never again become a political tool that spreads disunity and drives a wedge between Zimbabweans. Politicized ethnicity encourages the people of Zimbabwe to remain immature, unable to grieve, and move on by burying their past. Using this song as a reminder of a painful past that is treated as a period in the past without resuscitating it in manipulative political power aspirations, both the Ndebele and Shona people of Zimbabwe should reward Gwenyambira for passing on a valuable piece of history.

Nhemamusasa should also be examined in terms of the more excellent African experience, which spans continents, uniting the expressions of African identity through music and conveying those experiences. Patterns of communication demonstrating the uniqueness of African existence, whether under inter-tribal conflicts, slavery, or colonial subjugation, are expressed through song and dance because this is at the core of African nature to sing and dance. Nhemamusasa exudes these themes and experiences in its stanzas.

In Nhemamusasa, there are styles and use of language that resonates with the African American experiences, which are also expressed in song. Limiting Nhemamusasa to just a hunting song or makeshift shelters restricts a whole genre of music to a superficial rendition. Yet, the song encapsulates so much more of the African experience that is both Zimbabwean and continental in expression and content. This is why similar patterns are found across seas wherever you find people of African descent, even if they have been separated for long periods. For starters, it is essential to examine why Nhemamusasa brings the Shona woman to the fore in the celebration of marriage, a lamentation over the poor quality of a wife or wedding, and the dynamics of family relations. All these aspects are reflected in the two artists that sing the song. These are Chiwoniso Maraire and Ambuya Beauler Dyoko.

There was no specific reason for choosing the two artists who happened to be women because many artists and groups have recorded Nhemamusasa. Stella Chiweshe, one of the mbira greats, recorded various versions of Nhemamusasa with great mbira vocals.

It is essential to shedding some light on why the Shona woman features in Nhemamusasa, a song that belongs to what can be termed an old world in literature. This is long before feminism and the fight for gender equality. Nhemamusasa emphasizes the

Shona woman more than other aspects of the song. That begs the question, why is that so?

Language is carefully crafted to convey the women as the song's main focus without identifying any particular woman. There are various reasons why the music was presented in that manner.

# Chapter 4

## Shona Language

In examining the lyrics of the song *Nhemamusasa,* it is imperative to understand some fundamentals of the characteristics of the Shona language and the time that gave birth to the music.

Shona is spoken by the majority of the people of Zimbabwe as one of the major languages, followed by Ndebele, which is one of the Nguni languages of South Africa. Shona has many dialects, which also define the different subgroups of people found in parts of Zimbabwe. The sixteen dialects, mostly Karanga, Korekore, Budya, Zezuru, Maungwe, Manyika, Ndau, and many others, reflect divergent practices that characterize these subgroups. However, Shona is the primary language that brings all the subgroups together. When examining the origin of Shona as a language, scholars say there is no language called Shona like Yoruba, Zulu, or Herero. Still, it is a name initially used to identify people who lived in the area or region where the sun sets. With time, it was applied as the collective name of the different tribes of a particular region. In other words, it could be argued that the origin of the name Shona is Nguni because southern tribes referred to the people in the Mashonaland region as those from the area where the sun sets- *ama-Tshona*. Ama-Tshona- *people from where the sun sets.*

Then another school of thought postulates that there was an area inhabited by the Shona today where the Sona animal was abundant. From that association, the area earned the name *Sona* which later evolved into an identity of the people who lived in the place where the animal called Sona was found.

Yet, another school of thought says the word Shona is an adulteration of Senna. For example, Musina in South Africa is also derived from Mu-Senna.

Interestingly, recent research suggests the origin of the Shona language is associated with the Lost Tribes of Israel in southern Africa. Tudor Parfitt, a British researcher, links parts of the Shona language to some Yemenite dialects. In one of the interviews in a Video Home Service aired on PBS in 2000, Shona borrowed its origin from some Yemenite idioms. For instance, the *Va-* prefix denoting plural or honorific plural is actually of Yemenite derivation.

In Shona, we say *mu-* nhu (mu- prefix denoting singular reference for a person – mu-nhu).

Then its variations can be *chi-nhu (chi-* diminutive reference); There is also *zvi-nhu* ( zvi-denoting quantity), and lastly, *hu-nhu (*a state of being that is of good quality)

*Mu-* nhu (singular for person)

*Va-* nhu (plural for more than one person)

*Va-* prefix also denotes honorific reference, and the plural means more than one person; for example, Va- She (the king)- honorific plural.

Va- kuru (the elder)- honorific plural

Va- vhimi (Many hunters)

Va- rimi (many or several farmers)

In Tudor Parfitt's research, it turns out that while the Shona language structure uses the *Va-* prefix to denote plural and honor as part of its nineteen noun classes, Yemenite dialects also have the same structure to identify a group of people or plural forms like *Va- Sadiki, or Va- Tovakare, Va- Shavi.*

I mention this to make the reader understand that the argument that no original language called Shona could be actual because what is referred to as the Shona language structure borrows from other languages in the Middle East. This unclear origin of the Shona language leaves sub-groups of the Shona to stand out as distinct tribes identified by their languages, which were later incorporated into a structured form called the Shona language.

References to foreign dialects as far afield as Yemen mean that Shona has borrowed and included many words from other languages to make up the language that we call Shona today through the evolution and dynamism of language. Different subgroups have contributed to the development of the language in the expression of customs and beliefs over the years.

Terence Ranger points out that the move to come up with Shona as a language started with missionaries in Manicaland who wanted to document local dialects into a common language acceptable to all tribes to facilitate the preaching of the gospel. Ranger and David Beach concur that the Shona people were only conscious of the local chieftaincy group rather than a broader governmental system that brought the tribes together under a system of governance. Still, the numerous groups were never clustered together in self-conscious ethnicities, as implied by the term Manyika, Zezuru, and others. The Portuguese used the word Zezuru to describe people who lived around the head of Mazowe Valley, and it meant "people who live in a high area" Ndau was a derogatory term used on people of the eastern frontier by the raiding Gaza Nguni in the mid-nineteenth century.

The colonialists used tribal names to convey a sense of tribal identity and affiliation.

The Portuguese developed the concept of Manyika, claiming that Mutasa had voluntarily submitted to them, but the British challenged the idea.

Missionaries had a different approach to the development of Shona as a collective identity of a group of people in Zimbabwe. Helen Springer, in 1903 wrote, "We never forget that the primary object of our work here is to give the native the bible and enable him to read it" There was a need for a common language that could be used to proselytize the different tribes that comprise present-day Shona people. A common language in written form was a powerful tool for missionary influence.

Yet, another group had a capitalist approach to uniting the ethnic dialects because, with the advent of the printing press, more literature could be sold to a broader audience. As such, it was essential to unite the different dialects into one language to broaden the consumer base of the printed materials in one language spoken by many.

There was another problem. The question of who Shona is has presented a challenge, as people in present-day Zimbabwe were also known as VaNyai or BaNyai.

David Beach mentions in the *Addendorff or BaNyailand Trekk* that present-day Zimbabwe was the land of VaNyai or BaNyai. The term Nyai-

derives from *Munyai- meaning messenger or servant.*
Historians point out that people living between the
Zambezi and Limpopo had distinguished themselves
in their ability to use diplomacy in their relationship
with outsiders, which earned them the name VaNyai.
The name VaNyai is also mentioned by Solomon
Mutsvairo in his Shona novel *Feso.* Mutsvairo slots in
a poem that begins with the line *"Kuchazove riiniko isu
VaNyai tichitambudzika zvakadai…?- For how long shall
we, VaNyai, continue to suffer like this?"* The people
referred to in the book are present-day Shona people
who were called VaNyai then.

Even a religious hymn in Shona called *Wauya
Mucheki* talks about the return of Jesus Christ to the
earth accompanied by messengers of heaven who are
termed *vaNyai veDenga* (Messengers of Heaven) in
the song. All this helps to define the geographic
limits of the areas of Zimbabwe, where
Nhemamusasa was sung as a pass time, lament, and
in ritual ceremonies.

While there are no recorded acts in which
VaNyai diplomatic skills were demonstrated, Shona
registers, distinct forms of communication, can be
viewed as a residue of a one-time robust diplomatic
language. Ngano is one such example, which, apart
from being a pass-time storytelling register, carries a
deliberately constructed mode of communication
designed to foster peace in a community by

minimizing conflict through confrontation. Ngano is a register of peace and harmony, which Nhemamusasa borrows heavily from. The ability to transmit such forms of speech orally, without any documentation before colonization, says a lot about how Shona people valued the forms of speech they may have used in peaceful interactions with outsiders. Nhemamusasa can be viewed as another communication coded to relay particular messages.

# Chapter 5

## Multiple meanings of words in Shona

Shona is known for having words with more than one meaning as well as alterations made by voice pitch. It is characterized by intonations that can distinguish the meaning of a word spelled the same way.

Intonation in speech is changing (rising and falling) vocal pitch to convey grammatical information or personal attitude. Like in spoken English, where intonation is used to express questions, in Shona, intonation can express attitude, feeling of anger, and joy and the true meaning or instruction being given through the inflection used. Chiwoniso repeats Nhemamusasa in her rendition for emphasis to draw the attention of Nhemamusasa, who could have been absorbed in watching the sun, probably in winter. The use of *'Iwe Nhemamusasa'* singles him out as the focus of the message in a manner that is understood and accepted by other people who may be around.

*Nhemamusasa*

*Nhemamusasa*

*Wakaringe zuva nhamo ichauya iwe*

*Iwe Nhemamusasa*

*Nhemamusasa*

Inflection is the practice of inserting emphasis into your words. In linguistics, the study of how words are formed (morphology), inflection is a process of word formation in which a comment is modified to express different grammatical categories. All these dynamics of language impact the understanding and interpretation of the traditional song Nhemamusasa.

The dualism of meaning in Shona is expressed through inflections which play a significant role in denoting the definition of a word.

In Nhemamusasa, two words are joined together to form a meaning which is 1) *nhema-* and 2) *musasa.* When separated, the two words can convey other meanings.

For instance, *nhema-* has many meanings:

> a)     To begin with, it is derived from the verb *tema- meaning to cut something or the color black.*
> b)     *As part of Nhemamusasa, nhema- is a linking verb* expressing the cutting of tree branches to

make a shelter by probably more than one person. Communal activities like nhemamusasa, collectively called nhimbe or cooperatives, were and are still common in the Shona culture. There could have been other activities that fell under the nhemamusasa practice, like marriage ceremonies and hunting. *From* the expression of the term Nhemamusasa, there is also an implied meaning that this practice is habitual.

c) *Nhema- can also mean lies (*an assertion that is believed to be false, typically used to deceive someone)

d) *Nhema - black in color.*

e) *It also has a variation dema-which carries an emphasis on blackness in a derogatory manner. Tema* for black color, or to cut

f) *Nhema- a name of a wild animal called rhinoceros*

*Musasa,* on the other hand, can mean a temporary shelter or an indigenous tree commonly found in the bush veldts of Africa with the biological name *Brachystegia spiciform.*

The person analyzing the song Nhemamusasa needs to understand the whole meaning of the two combined words to convey the proper sense. This is because Nhemamusasa can also mean gathering people together to help set up a new home, especially for a son who has come of age and married. The elders come together to mark a particular spot as the site of the plot or lot for the new settlement. Usually, the father of the settler drills a peg on the location of the new home to make the new house a recognized entity in the family and community because the head of the house, which in this case is the father of the settler or the oldest brother has formalized the setting up of the new settlement. The term *nhemamusasa*, in this case, connotes an action that more than one person will do as a sign of communal support for the ones starting a new home. Elders call it nhemamusasa because a home is a shelter. Nhema- derived from the verb *kutema* or tema, which means to cut out branches, can also mean a community ceremony in which the elder of a family lead in demarcating a new lot, and the rest of the community renders their support in cutting trees for the new home. Some form of festivity usually marks such a ceremony, be it alcohol drinking, food, or even a more significant celebration. However, in the grand scheme of things, every home, no matter how beautiful, is temporary in some way because we do not live forever. Hence the term musasa for temporary shelter denotes the transient nature of humanity's stay in any given place.

The two words *nhema-* and *musasa-* are married to form a different combination: the one who makes temporary shelter. Even that needs to be expanded to express that Nhemamusasa felled trees to create a temporary shelter. This implies that the person is not sedentary but engages in makeshift shelters.

On the one hand, Nhemamusasa can be viewed in the context of the old-world Shona poetry anthology and song in which shifting cultivation is practiced. The song also corrects the person still making a temporary shelter to cease living a nomadic life and be sedentary because *ukaringe zuva nhamo ichauya iwe.* A warning from concerned onlookers to a lazy person. Could Nhemamusasa be a victim of prevailing conflict that causes him to move from place to place? Being on the run to escape from something that Gwenyambira is not comfortable enough to disclose. In the face of destabilization, the only thing left for Nhemamusasa is to watch the sun as it rises and sets. Nhemamusasa could be a character specially chosen to depict the behavior of an internally displaced community. And Gwenyambira is calling on the community to focus on settling down despite the prevailing confusion. Accepting passively, the disruption of their lives will only lead to more woes- *nhamo ichauya.* There are many facets of the challenges faced by Shona communities that Gwenyambira has captured through the song. It is clear that Nhemamusasa is unstable, and Gwenyambira hints at why in coded speech.

There is also a historical context for the song Nhemamusasa in Shona folklore. It is vital to go beyond the surface meaning of the song, which calls for a closer examination of the Shona folklore from which the Nhemamusasa song originates.

## Chapter 6

### Influence of Ngano Folklore on Nhemamusasa

In the Shona language, *ngano-* folklore falls within a specific style of speech known as a register. A register is a variety of languages used for a particular purpose or communicative situation. Ngano's specific form and style aim to inform, entertain, and relay didactic elements of Shona folklore, which target the audience. It was and still is a significant contributor to social stability by addressing social deviants openly through story and song without confrontation. Understanding this oral relaying of information from generation to generation makes the listener understand the wealth of customs and traditions encapsulated in a few verses of Nhemamusasa.

From the renditions of Nhemamusasa, there are aspects of folklore in both Chiwoniso Maraire and Ambuya Beauler Dyoko versions. Ngano is one poignant aspect of the Shona language, which explains why the Shona people could have earned the name VaNyai. It is a communication register employed for conflict resolution using diplomatic means to address social problems. By coming up with Ngano as a mature language that promotes social harmony, the VaNyai or Shona people established conflict resolution, mediation, and peaceful existence measures well before the United Nations was born. They were skilled diplomats. While relations between nations and states changed before and during the song's time, Ngano and Nhemamusasa are residues of a once robust means of communication by a group of people with diplomatic skills called VaNyai- Messengers. Nhemamusasa employs ngano-style structures in both renditions.

## Structure of Ngano

In ngano, you have the **sarungano-storyteller**, the **vateereri-audienc**e, who respond to the storyteller in a specific way. In the mbira genre of Shona culture, you have **gwenyambira/**

**mushauri**- the thumb piano player and the lead singer and **vatsinhiri/ vabvumiri**- backup singers.

**Ngano structure comprises:**

Sarungano- storyteller

Vateereri- audience

**Form of Ngano:** Sarungano starts the narration by saying, **"Kwaivepo"- Once upon a time.**

The audience/ vateereri then responds by saying, **"Dzepfunde."**

The ngano ends with **Ndopakafira sarungano- This is where the storyteller died.**

**Purpose of Ngano**

To entertain, educate, inform, and correct any negative behavior or attitude without confrontation to avoid conflict in interpersonal and community relations.

Within the ngano story is usually a song and possible dance by the listeners who are led in music by the storyteller. There can be clapping of hands and dance too.

The singing and dancing are meant to keep the listeners engaged and to emphasize the point of the story so that vateereri /listeners can quickly grasp the message being relayed because, in most cases, the story is being told to address an ongoing problem within the community and the person at fault may be present among the listeners. In other words, there is fun with a purpose.

To end the story, the sarungano says, **"Ndopakaperera sarungano or ndipo pakafira sarungano"- "This is where this storyteller ended.**

Or **this is where the storyteller died."**

This implies that the storyteller's version ends or dies. Still, the story continues and will be told by another storyteller to convey relevant elements to a particular audience in the future.

The concept of didactic elements in Ngano stories is at the center of the story's carefully crafted pattern of flow and carefully chosen words to drive the point home. You find the same elements in Nhemamusasa, which in storytelling would be a part of the song and not a stand-alone piece.

In Nhemamusasa, some elements conform the song to Shona folklore.

**Mushauri/the lead singer** who sets the pitch and tone of the song in the two renditions, are Chiwoniso and Ambuya Beauler Dyoko.

**Mutsinhiri (singular)/ Vatsinhiri (plural)** - the backup singers

Dance and the playing of mbira- thumb piano accompanies the voices

The singing in both Ngano and Nhemamusasa is categorized into two sections. The first one is called **kushaura- to lead in a song,** which is the lead singer's role. In Nhemamusasa, Gwenyambira, or mbira player, is the lead singer in the rendition of Chiwoniso. She has backup voices that sing and ululate while. Ambuya Beauler Dyoko's performance in New York has her as a soloist.

**Backup singers are called vatsinhiri,** who plays the role of kutsinhira- to back up a song.

Ngano and Nhemamusasa have an entertainment focus built within them called kutandara/ kukwedzisa or relaxation, which has an ingrained element of wisdom speech and carefully selected words that sound good to the ear as driving the intended point home to the target person or audience.

Stella Chiweshe takes on a purely Ngano style in her version of Nhemamusasa. She talks of famine and the need to journey to a fruitful place- Maroro, alluding to the nomadic nature of ancient Shona and other tribes in search of food and water during droughts. Her version is a lamentation over the effects of starvation. - *Makanga masara muri vangani gore rino nzara. Ndoita, Seiko ini?*

*Pandinoenda, ndokudambura, ndoenda newe ini*

*Pasi kwenyika maroro*

Chiweshe's rendition takes on the structure of ngano, in which mystery is part of the unfolding story. She says that the sun is rising from where it sets- *zuva rinobuda nekumadokero*

Mbuya Beauler Dyoko, in her rendition from the Album *Afamba Apota,* in which Cosmas Magaya accompanies her, talks about the bitterness of fallen heroes- *Shungu dzemagamba akatisiya*

*Hatidi kuona zvimhingamupinyi mberi kwedu- we do not want to see hurdles in people's paths. Presumably, according to the song, these hurdles* are put in the way of the living by the spirits of the dead, who perished in the war, and nothing has been done to bury their remains with honor.

Ambuya Beauler Dyoko, and Cosmas, present a contemporary Nhemamusasa, which fears that the spirits of fallen heroes of the Second Chimurenga would cause instability in a free country because they were not appeased. This draws the listener to a version of a contemporary Nhemamusasa that seeks to call the attention of authorities in government to address the issue of the burial of foreign heroes of the Liberation Struggle for Zimbabwe (Second Chimurenga)

All these are versions of Nhemamusasa that prove that they come from a genre with situational lyrics coined for the situation by the ingenuity of Gwenyambira. They express information about what is going on at a particular time: starvation, marriage ceremony celebration, the fear of impending danger, or the dangers of flouting traditional rites in Shona culture. Most of these elements are employed in Ngano.

Entertainment was for children and older adults as family and community interacted with all age groups in the evenings and kept the children engaged until bedtime. The correction was made in a general manner so that individuals would have sense enough to correct their errant behavior. Ngano also taught wisdom as children began to understand the difference between good and bad behavior, as represented by the animal kingdom. Storytelling was an art that often required the storyteller to think "on the go" as they pooled words that would convey the desired meaning so that the intended target of the message would get it.

Ngano, in particular, was told during harvest times when people are roasting nuts and corn and eating pumpkins, which are all seasonal crops that signal that the season has yielded good harvests by the availability of all the above. The atmosphere is full of hope and celebration. This is the opposite of the times of drought when villagers would have to depend on roots and berries for survival. Stella Chiweshe echoes the effects of drought on the population in her rendition of Nhemamusasa. In essence, many things are celebrated in Ngano and folk music encapsulated in a few lines of a verse or the articulation of the storyteller. There is hope and bliss in the atmosphere and every reason to celebrate. The Shona people know that life is made up of a tapestry of change and surprises like an invasion by marauding tribes, wildfires, and storms that could decimate lives. The old world in which Nhemamusasa was sung was full of uncertainty; as a result, the Shona wove in celebrations of harvests, the new moon, and marriages with song and dance with full knowledge of the fate of life. These elements are expressed in both Ngano and Nhemamusasa. There was and still is sorrow even in times of celebration, as the examination of Mbuya Beauler Dyoko reveals.

Ngano is a part of Shona registers devised to make communication easier among different relationship groups. Apart from ngano, other registers are relational, like Chiramu, Chisahwira, Chivhevhano, or Kupfimbana/ Courtship, to mention a few not relevant to this book. These registers were meant to ease communication between people of the opposite sex in a family or community setting. Regarding Ngano, it is a structured style of communication in which there is a sarungano- the storyteller and the audience. The two groups have roles throughout the session. The sarungano starts with *Kwaivapo- Once upon a time*. The audience responds by saying *Dzepfunde*. After the audience responds, the storytellers can gauge alertness and interest. The ngano storytelling is akin to the western world's cartoon characters and animation in which animals speak like human beings. That fascinates children who begin to understand that even wild animals used in the storytelling represent certain types of characteristics of people in real life but are also in awe of knowing that animals speak. For example, using the baboon and hare or rabbit in a Ngano denotes that the baboon is big but unwise, yet the hare is small but active and clever. The storyteller in Ngano employs song and sometimes dances to emphasize the point that must be addressed. The Ngano register has characteristics that belie the whole narration. There is a didactic element all the time.

## History of animation and cartoon characters

Shona culture aims to teach the children using familiar elements from the local environment. With a very close connection with the wild, Shona people grew very familiar with the characteristics of the animals in their environment. Everyone knows the animal's characteristics when a Shona person describes an individual as 'tsuro' / hare/ rabbit. If a person is likened to such an animal, then they know the person's personality traits. Animals were long employed in storytelling in Shona culture before animation in cartoons. The storyteller would depict the baboon as a thief in the story as a way of teaching the children that theft is not tolerated in society, but this was put across in a way that was not offensive. Most of the time, there would be culprits in the audience who would have stolen from others or committed a crime in the community. Instead of publicly humiliating them, the elders then told a story that used animals that mimic the behavior of the offenders so that the individuals would identify their mistake in the Ngano and hopefully correct their behavior without being made public ridicule.

## Chapter 7

## Nhemamusasa, a Mbira Genre

Nhemamusasa falls within the Mbira traditional Shona genre of music. Mbira is a musical instrument called a thumb piano which is commonly played in Southern Africa, especially in Mozambique and Zimbabwe. It has been found as far away from Africa as the Caribbean. Other traditional songs and dances like Mhande, Shangara, Chinyamusasure, and Jerusarema combine dance, singing, the drum, and other conventional instruments.

Although there is a limited anthology of Shona traditional music from the past, it is easy to piece together similarities that indicate relationships between music and Ngano. While many writers have written interesting scripts about Nhemamusasa focusing on hunting and entertainment, Nhemamusasa is a genre of mbira music, if not the mbira music genre of the Shona people. Just like in Ngano oral transmission, Nhemamusasa has many variations in its rendition; if one takes two examples of Chiwoniso Maraire and Ambuya Beauler Dyoko that are commenting on what is obtaining at a particular time in a community. The two renditions reveal that Nhemamusasa is a genre of mbira in which the Gwenyambira plays the role of social commentator about marriage ceremonies, quality of marriage, military prowess, hunting skills, and interaction with the spirit world. On the other hand, Stella Chiweshe in *Njuzu* – Nhemamusasa is talking about the marine world, but it is still a version of Nhemamusasa. It is a self-contained genre that comments on what society was going through at a particular season among the Shona people. Nhemamusasa is about a community and how people view their daily lives and express their views of correction and wishes through music. To limit Nhemamusasa to a single song would be to deny a whole genre of music its power and influence over the Shona people and how it shaped their interactions and general well-being.

Nowadays, mbira instruments and music are solemnized as mbira dzavadzimu- *the mbira of the ancestors*. There could be some veracity to the claim because of the possible etymology of the word mbira. This is highly debatable because both Chiwoniso and even other mbira groups play the role of social commentators and use the instrument in traditional ceremonies. The disruption of Shona's lives could have necessitated this attachment during the early days of colonization when the settler government confiscated any item or artifact that symbolized unity or power among the Shona after colonization to weaken Shona's resistance. This was also coupled with some of the missionary teachings that proclaimed anything African, or in this case, Shona traditional practice, was evil, and mbira and drums were banned in some denominations. Most likely, the preservation of mbira had to be reinforced by attaching it to Shona tradition as the instrument of the ancestors because venerated ancestors like Chaminuka had played the instrument. However, that should not limit the use of the instrument in church or outside because before the mbira was designated as the ancestors' instrument, it was a musical instrument that could be used in performance on any platform among both the Shona and non-Shona artists. This should not, however, take away the sacred nature in which the Shona people view the instrument.

# Chapter 8

## Comparisons and similarities of Chiwoniso and Ambuya Beauler's renditions of the first verses

### Chiwoniso says in her version of Nhemamusasa;

Mhururu- ululation

Hiya

Hiya hah

Hoo- horendere hiya

Hiya

Hiya- hah

Hoo-horendere hiya

Hiya

Hiya wore e

Woo-horendere hiya

Nhemamusasa

Nhemamusasa

Wakaringe zuva iwe nhamo ichauya iwe

Iwe Nhemamusasa

Nhemamusasa

Wakaringe zuva nhamo ichauya

     In celebration, Chiwoniso Maraire introduces the song with ululation and mahon'era to set the atmosphere for the audience to prepare for merriment, and the depth of meaning carried in the music. Then when she says *Pereka, pereka, pereka, pereka mvura mukaranga iwe,* it becomes clear that this type of Nhemamusasa is a celebration of a new bride undertaking all the standard requirements at the start of a marriage. She also highlights the importance of time and its impact on poverty if not appropriately managed. However, the 'nhamo' mentioned by Chiwoniso has more than one meaning. *Nhamo ichauya* is a warning of poor safety or security more than the *nhamo/ poverty* of not finding something to eat because Nhemamusasa wasted time- *wakaringe zuva nhamo ichauya iwe!*

     Again *nhamo/problem/predicament* can also refer to a dilemma that is not necessarily poverty. The multiple meanings of Shona words can convey many messages which have nothing to do with poverty but other social challenges. This euphemistic term is employed to relay that Nhemamusasa should not be lazy. This is a perfect example of the "ngano" style presentation of harsh messages in a softened or palatable tone to the message's target. In this case, lyrics tell Nhemamusasa to be more diligent about life. The way it is employed in the song makes Nhemamusasa a generic name to avoid pinpointing an actual person. As a result, one can argue that Nhemamusasa was a collective term for social commentary through song among the Shona people. Anyone can be Nhemamusasa in this genre.

Ambuya Beauler Dyoko, who sings the same song as a lamentation, brings in a somber atmosphere of bloodshed. It needs to be clarified whether the act is on a battlefield or a hunting experience. There are undertones of scorn, and disdain in the statement, whether it is from the victim or an onlooker, The scorn is directed at the one holding the arrow. The victim or onlooker despises the one holding the weapon- *Roverera museve, hanzvadzi yamai vako zvaisingarime.*

*Kuroora roora ndaroora nguruve,*

*Hanzvadzi yamai vako zvaisingarime*

*Hiya woye woyere ona*

## Mbuya Beauler Dyoko' rendition of Nhemamusasa:

*Roverera museve*

*Hanzvadzi yamai vako zvaisingarime*

*Roverera museve*

*Kuroora roora ndaroora nguruve,*

*Hanzvadzi yamai vako zvaisingarime*

*Hiya woye*

*woyere onaa*

*Hanzvadzi yamai vako zvaisingarime*


*Kuroora ndaroora nguruve*

*Hanzvadzi yamai vako zvaisingarime*

*Iya*

*woiye*

*worende heya*

Roverera museve ona

Roverera museve

Kuroora roora ndaroora nguruve

Hanzvadzi yamai vako zvaisingarime


Kuroora, roora ndaroora humba ini.

Iya Woye

Awo

Woyere hona

Iye woye a

Woiyere awoye

Awona  wauya

Hanzvadzi yamai vako zvaisingarime

Kuroora roora ndarooranguruve

Hanzvadzi yamai vako zvaisingarime

Iya woire woyere hona

Hanzvadzi yamai vako zvaisingrime

*Kuroora ndaroora nguruve*

*Hani, Changamire*

*Changamire x 5*

Both artists render the same piece carrying the same message using different lyrics employed situationally, and the meter is harnessed to reflect the mood.

Chiwoniso introduces Nhemamusasa with mhururu-ululation to tell the audience that the song is about jubilation and celebration. It could be at a traditional marriage ceremony. After singling out Nhemamusasa to quit a lazy lifestyle- *kuringe zuva nhamo ichauya iwe*, Chiwoniso then delves into what appears to be the focus of the celebration.

*Pereka, Pereka, Pereka,*

*Pereka, pereka, pereka, pereka mvura mukaranga iwe*

*Pereka, Pereka, Pereka,*

*Pereka, pereka, pereka, pereka mvura mukaranga iwe*

This verse of Nhemamusasa is ethno-focused because it brings in the Korekore dialect in which *kupereka mvura* is to give water or anything to somebody reverently, mainly to an esteemed person or an elder. In this case, it is a process of the marriage ceremony in which the bride has to fulfill certain rites in a ceremonial gesture as a newly married woman introduces herself to the new family of her husband by giving water to all the members of the family for both drinking, and bathing then she applies special oils on them. The ceremony is called washing/bathing the family; the bride starts from the oldest to the youngest members of the new family. In turn, those who go through the symbolic process of being bathed by the new wife respond by giving her money or other gifts. Again, the family gathers for such a ceremony because the bride is received as a daughter-in-law and as a mother who will care for all the members, whether young or old. To demonstrate her kindness and love, she bathes all the members present and cooks for them, cleans up the yard, and fetches water. All these are the chores that a new wife is expected to undertake for the rest of her life as a mother of the whole family and her children. The bride must demonstrate these strengths when she joins her husband's family. Here is where Chiwoniso and Ambuya Beauler's renditions converge or tie in regarding the marriage process. If the bride is lazy, it will be apparent during the day that she undertakes the house chores of bathing the family members, fetching wood, cooking, and serving the food all in one day. The elders, especially the matriarchs, watch for cues that show whether a woman is diligent or lazy by how she will perform on the first day in the new family. Remember, also, that the brides of yesteryear were still teenagers, and to pull such an elaborate initial introduction into a family was daunting and lazy women would break down or undercook food or even break the pitchers on their way from the well to fetch water. With time, it would become clear that the bride may not be the best choice made by the son, and that reflects poorly on the son, who then laments that "Yes, I am married, but she is nothing but a pig- *Kuroora roora ndaroora nguruve*" "*Kuroora, roora ndaroora humba*" **humba**, *and* **nguruve** are synonyms for *'pig'* in Shona. It is important to remember that statements uttered in the song by Gwenyambira were not limited to a single meaning. However, the audience understood the dimensions of meaning expressed in the music.

Due to the celebratory nature of Chiwoniso's rendition, the bride is referred to as **mukaranga**, an endearing word for a wife or young bride. Chiwoniso is urging her to present the water to the family because such occasions were challenging for the young girl who had left all that was familiar in her family to join strangers who, at times, did not treat her sparingly but expected her to show maturity in all that she did, even if she was only a teenager. The first encounter must have been brutal, but the urging tone in Chiwoniso is both encouraging and reassuring to the bride- *Pereka Pereka Pereka pereka pereka mvura mukaranga iwe*

The incident depicted in Chiwoniso's piece is a typical practice of the rites of passage for the new wife in Shona culture.

In contrast, Ambuya Beauler Dyoko starts with the hunting chant or war cry but immediately reverts to the role of the commentator on the quality of relationships in a community. However, she introduces an essential aspect of the Shona life in that dispensation, the Nguni raids on the Shona people, especially in parts of present-day Mashonaland.

 Mbuya Beauler Dyoko is in a pensive mood. Her rendition of Nhemamusasa includes a war cry, hunting chant, and lament.

Roverera museve- *thrust the arrow without reservation.*

This is not clear whether a rookie in warfare is being given the order to release an arrow toward the enemy or a young hunter is being ordered to kill the prey without regard for how he may feel if it's the first time to see life departing from a body, because that is his source of livelihood. The reason for the young to be aggressive with the arrow is that the mother's brother does not care to till the land and offer him an alternative lifestyle. In other words, the young man has a defunct support system that calls for him to learn survival skills as soon as possible. The commentator urges Nhemamusasa to develop his skills to make a livelihood by fighting in battle or hunting.

The following line is a lament over a marriage- *Kuroora roora ndaroora nguruve*. In this lament of regretting a marriage in which the wife is not clean or hygienic, the Gwenyambira- the piano player is pouring out their pain before the community. Again, euphemism reflects the quality of a woman the man married; *a pig- filthy woman*. The repetitive pattern- *Kuroora, roora, ndaroora nguruve*, and then *Kuroora ndaroora ndaroora humba* serves to capture the listener's ear so that they can aptly relate *roora*- marriage and the curve-pig. When the word *nguruve* is mentioned, the listener is aware of the message's essence.

Ambuya Beauler Dyoko is panting with pain as a social commentator as she brings out the problem of poverty in a society that lives off of the land. Furthermore, the married man in the community has no marital bliss because the wife does not please him.

Here is the power of the Shona culture to handle stress and domestic disputes. The song becomes the medium of expression in addressing social issues and an outlet for the pain of the person going through marital problems. The problem is for more than just the two people involved; it becomes a problem for the community to know of and address. This is expressed in the Shona proverb- *Mbudzi kuzvarira pavanhu hunzi nditandirwe imbwa.* The literal translation is that when a goat decides to give birth in people's presence, it expects them to chase away dogs that may want to attack her young. In Shona, the proverb means that when a person makes public their problems, it is in the hope that the community will help resolve them together with them. So, the Nhemamusasa genre depicts these characteristics of standard practices among the Shona.

After releasing the words of pain, Ambuya Beauler uses mahon'era to give the audience time to digest what gwenyambira (Ambuya Beauler) has just said.

The common denominator of both renditions of Nhemamusasa is that music is a medium of expression employed to present the mood, condition, and even the struggles of day-to-day living.

Apart from pushing the Shona woman to the forefront, there are other aspects, like evoking the spirit realm. This is expressed by Ambuya Beauler Dyoko more than Chiwoniso Maraire.

## Chapter 9

## Language of War in Nhemamusasa

Times of conflict influence the development of language that relays messages for safety and security without enemy detection. In Nhemamusasa, there is a description of *nhamo ichauya/ impending peril* that needs to be defined. The term *nhamo i*s good enough to arouse concern in the audience being addressed. Watching the sunrise and the set is a pass time engagement done by those who are at ease. Times have changed, and Gwenyambira warns Nhemamusasa to adjust to the change. In other words, there could have been times when Shona people could afford the luxury of watching the sun without any safety concerns. In Nhemamusasa, there is a transition requiring hyper-vigilance. Still, Nhemamusasa may be adjusting poorly to the changes, risking his life by trying to hold on to old ways. Nhemamusasa could also be a code name employed in the lyrics representing any community resident. The audience understands who is being referred to when mentioning Nhemamusasa. The Nguni tribes' invasion of the area now called Mashonaland lends the most plausible explanation for the difficult transition that Nhemamusasa is experiencing from a time of safety to hazardous conditions.

Satire is employed in both renditions to convey the message of an unstable political system in which the Shona people went through incessant raids from the Nguni groups and other local raiders. The first three lines refer to the Nguni style of raiding and their lives not characterized by farming. The satire is directed at the groups like the internally recruited Dumbuseya, who carried out Nguni-style raids, which they learned from Ngwana Masesenyane's group, which had recruited them from Nyajena, the Ndebele state, based at Bulawayo, Zwangendaba's plundering across the land of present-day Zimbabwe, on his way north. It may have been hard for ordinary villagers to distinguish between the groups because they used similar tactics in their fight and plundering styles. The villagers may not have known when an attack would come their way, so the song makes it clear *"Iwe Nhemamusasa, usaringe zuva nhamo ichauya iwe"* However, when the attack came on unarmed villagers, then Ambuya Beauler Dyoko, expresses, the sight, and the emotions of onlookers, who could have been in hiding.

*Roverera museve*

*Hanzvadzi yamai vako zvaisingarime*

*Roverera museve*

Ambuya Beauler Dyoko stands out as she seeks to distinguish a particular arrow used for combat in inter-tribal wars and hunting. However, just as in ngano, where words are crafted to convey more than the surface meaning, Ambuya Beauler Dyoko could be referring to a particular incident of Nguni raids in the first verses of her rendition of Nhemamusasa. Here is the reason why? *Roverera museve* suggests a close encounter in battle, hunting, or even a fight. In hunting, such instruments as arrows were not close combat weapons, but knives were used to slit the throat of an animal that had been darted already. The verse here suggests human combat. The Nguni tribes, with their assegais, engaged in a close battle with their foes or victims of raids. For instance, in 2018, I attended a church conference where one woman told a story about a Nguni impi that ripped apart her great-grandfather. She said the local community near Gweru still remembered the history of her grandfather's death. She said the family eventually exhumed his remains and gave him a decent burial. Her grandfather's attackers were Ndebele. Yet, that cannot be ascertained because other Nguni groups, Zwangendaba, Masesenyane, and the incorporated Dumbuseya, could have been responsible for such a heinous attack. The common name locals used was "Pfumo reDzviti" – the war of the Ndebeles, or the

Spear of the Ndebele" History, records those parts of the Midlands had many raiding and abducting groups that were not Ndebele.

It is also possible that Shona people may have loosely referred to assegais as arrows because that is the collective name that they knew for an unfamiliar weapon of war. There was no way that the Shona could have openly castigated the Nguni newcomers or any other raiding group, owing to their military superiority, except to carefully craft words that expressed the pain they may have witnessed as their cattle and daughters and sons were taken away. To the Gwenyambira, it may have mattered less who did the raiding because the results were either painful. Whether it was the Dumbuseya or Venda mercenaries who carried out the raids, Gwenyambira focuses on the pain witnessed and the possible loss of lives and seeks to give voice to their woes through Nhemamusasa. As the Shona endured this ordeal repeatedly, they used sarcasm to refer to raiders' actions during attacks- *Roverera museve, Hanzvadzi yamai vako zvaisingarime, Roverera museve.* The verse is disdainful of the act, but it sounds like it conveys encouragement to the killer, yet it is a helpless response to a brutal attack on those who cannot fight back.

It was the Mfecane raiders whom the Shona looked upon as lazy because they lived on raiding the weaker tribes around them hence *Hanzvadzi yamai vako zvaisingarime*. Solomon Mutsvairo, in *Chaminuka Prophet of Zimbabwe* (1983), echoes the same sentiments of Nguni laziness because the Shona people lived an agrarian life that was generally non-aggressive. Was the assertion that Nguni groups were lazy an accurate description of the band of impis? Not necessarily, because Nguni warriors were a band of men who had fled or migrated from Zululand. Some were just migratory, like the Zwangendaba Hlatshwayo and Jere people, who, despite migrating north, raided local communities in Mozambique and Zimbabwe and engaged in the slave trade. Depending on which Nguni group villagers had encountered during raids, it could very well be more vicious groups that assimilated both men and women into their ranks and took them away right before helpless fellow villagers. The Shona people, who were not warlike, were at the receiving end of the desperate Nguni impis and other local raiders, who continually abducted Shona women without mercy during incessant raids. The fear and confusion that was unleashed onto the Shona by these Nguni raids changed the Shona people forever. It was against Shona's decorum to engage in the abduction of women without accountability or the standard traditional practices of paying dowry, thereby establishing lasting family ties. On the other hand, Nguni influenced raids broke every known cultural norm among the Shona people, exposing their weakness in being unable to defend themselves against such tyranny. One only has to picture a Shona man pondering over what had become of his life as a man and a community member, as well as the dashed vision of the success of his family line and how those thoughts were expressed in the most familiar method of lamenting in song, both as an outlet for emotions as people were building temporary dwellings- *misasa* (plural for *musasa* - shelter) and communicating to his greater community the painful reality of war and raids and how life lost a sense of permanence.

The *nguruve/ humba/ pig* metaphor is a cry of the Shona man over his predicament of losing all the potential mothers of tomorrow being taken forcibly. It may have nothing to do with an unhygienic woman but an expression denoting the absence of the freedom to choose the woman that one loves or, even worse still, the total lack of young women suitable for marriage. The Shona man is lamenting the absence of freedom to love and choose a wife without limitation. In this case, the Gwenyambira has to accept that they may marry the weakest women in the community if there are any left because the good ones have been raided and abducted. In the eyes of the Gwenyambira, a pig can qualify for a wife due to the scarcity of young women. This expresses deep pain and a sense of loss articulated in the song. The loss of women from the Shona community right under the nose of their men who were supposed to protect them put the Shona men into a sense of emasculation. The only voice that the Shona man remained with was his voice accompanied by the thumb piano. There is an expression of deep-seated pain in Nhemamusasa by Dyoko. There is also a celebration and a festive mood of Nhemamusasa, by Chiwoniso.

Chiwoniso Maraire uses inflections in the last stanza to denote a warning. The same name Nhemamusasa is pronounced differently twice, as [Nhemamusasa] with a high pitch, and the second Nhemamusasa has a lower angle which carries a warning tone in Shona. In other words, even at the song's end, Maraire still has a warning message for Nhemamusasa to let the audience know that danger is still lurking.

Yet Ambuya Beauler Dyoko, who begins with a pensive mood, ends up in a celebratory tone as she interacts with spirits that announce their presence. The interaction with the spirit world is amply demonstrated by Dyoko's rendition- *Ndanzwa ngoma kurira. Kana uchitida togara pano maiwe!- I heard the sound of music or the beating of the drum. If you welcome us here, we will stay.* In other words, the playing of the mbira has beckoned the spirits of the dead to come to the party.

# Chapter 10

## Similarities between Negro Spirituals and aspects of Nhemamusasa

Euphemism is also employed in African American spirituals, where songs were used as cues among slave communications that their masters did not decipher. This is common in African American Negro spirituals during the Underground Railroad. Just like in Nhemamusasa, where some of the Shona groups were incapacitated in their quest to survive in the face of Nguni and internal raids, enslaved people had to employ a register that conveyed messages that were exclusive to the enslaved people to improve their chances of sending the right cues for what they needed to do, to escape from slave plantations. Negro spirituals were laments, chants of protest against the slave working and living conditions. The spirituals were adapted from their rich African heritage. Since enslavers forced enslaved people to go to church, their songs were biblically based but were coded messages expressing their pain and desire to escape and be free. Dr. James Norris, a professor of Music at Howard University and Director of Howard University Choir, points out that Negro spirituals had their roots in Africa, where music was infused in every aspect of life. Africans taken as enslaved from their motherland were not allowed to ply the instruments they brought, so they substituted that with clapping hands.

Terms like "*Old Satan*" were coded terms used in Negro spirituals to refer to the enslaver.

Phrases like *If you get there before I do, Tell all my friends I'm coming too,* were a sign of the readiness of enslaved people to escape to freedom. The power of song as a tool to convey coded messages expressing hope of freedom one day. And survival is an old and typically Black or African way of communicating difficult or painful messages with words that do not carry the tone of what is being conveyed. The chariot is a mode of transport, and when it swings low, it means a passenger needs to get on board. The enslaved people understood these codes.

*Swing low, sweet chariot.*

*Comin' for to carry me home;*

*Swing low, sweet chariot,*

*Comin' for to carry me home.*

*I looked over at Jordan,*

*And what did I see,*

*Comin' to carry me home…*

At face value, the lyrics carry a religious message of the Biblical Jordan River and angels coming for the saints. Yet, the message was about escaping enslaved people from the southern slave plantations to the north for freedom from bondage. The message's meaning was clear to black people, but the enslavers had no idea of the hidden meaning. This is the power of song and its diverse meanings as it was employed as an instrument of freedom from oppression, both on the African continent and in the diaspora.

The song "*Wade in the Water*" was used during Harriet Tubman's Underground Railroad, in which enslaved people escaping from the south to the north were being warned to avoid using dry land in their escape but to use waterways, where their scent could not be detected by dogs or slave catchers, could not sniff their trail. With time these songs of survival now form the genre of Negro spirituals, serving as a marker of the cultural identity of Africans who were forcibly taken out of Africa to the United States of America. Repetition is employed in Wade in the water and followed by the message, which is about God. *God's going to trouble the water.*

The African Americans depended on God to escape from the South through the Underground Railroads. God was not only going to trouble the waters, but sniffer dogs of enslavers would not be able to detect people crossing over or being tracked if they used waterways.

*See those people dressed in white.*

*They look like the children of the Israelites.*

Biblical redemption of Israelites from Egypt was employed to convey communication codes that sounded like the reciting of bible stories, yet, the people dressed in white, who looked like the children of Israel, were possibly rescuers bringing the messages of how to escape.

*See those people dressed in black.*

*They have come a long way, and they ain't turning back*

The above statement mentions the truth to encourage more people to develop the courage to run away and never look back. Just the courage to leave the plantation after witnessing the brutality meted out on those enslaved people who had attempted to escae before, and got caught must have needed much courage on from would-be escapees. Songs like *Wade in the waters*, counseled them to develop that courage, just like the children of Israel.

*Wade in the water*

*Wade in the water, children*

*Wade in the water*

*God's going to trouble the
water.*


*See those people dressed in
white*

*They look like the children of
the Israelites*


*Wade in the water*

*Wade in the water, children*

*Wade in the water*

*God's gonna trouble the water.*


*Wade in the water*

*Wade in the water, children*

*Wade in the water*

*God's gonna trouble the water.*

*See those people dressed in
black*

*They come a long way and they
ain't turning back*


*Wade in the water*

*Wade in the water, children*

*Wade in the water*

*God's gonna trouble the water.*


*See those people dressed in blue*

*Look like my people comin'
thru*


*Wade in the water*

*Wade in the water, children*

*Wade in the water*

*God's gonna trouble the water.*


*See those people dressed in red*

*Must be*
*the children that Moses led*


*Wade in the water*

*Wade in the water, children*

*Wade in the water*

*God's gonna trouble the water.*


*Some say Peter and some say*
*Paul*

*But there ain't but the one*
*God made us all.*


*Wade in the water*

*Wade in the water, children*

*Wade in the water*

*God's gonna trouble the water*

These songs conveyed more than one
meaning to enslaved people and to slave masters.
Yet we still sing them down through the years, yet at
some point they communicated messages of escape

and survival in the era of slavery. In the same manner, one can examine the Nhemamusasa genre as one that commentators used to talk about their environment, whether good or bad. The Shona despised a person who loathed working with their hands in the fields but to hide the actual meaning of the lyrics. For instance lyrics are rendered in a relational manner - *hanzvadzi yamai vako zvaisingarime.* The statement conveys the message of laziness. A mother's brother or uncle was a highly esteemed person in any family because he wore many hats, from counselor to material supporter for the sister or aunt's family during years of drought. With a strong family background full of brothers and uncles, a woman was secure in her marriage, and in life in general.

Although historians writing on Zimbabwe point out how missionaries forbade the use of local or traditional instruments, it should be noted that Europe had experienced a time where pianos, and other instruments were not allowed as part of worship. However, in Africa, and among the slaves, instruments were labeled as pagan, and that move conveyed messages that Africans were less than other human beings, hence there was no regard for what they valued or held in high esteem. Mbira as a musical instrument suffered the same fate during colonial times, as it was forbidden in the church. Its resurgence on the stage has been enhanced by mostly people who came from outside of Zimbabwe, who reinstated the instrument's worth and even popularity. The instrument remained important at traditional ceremonies or events, and among prominent families who held on to their traditional roots during the colonial era. For example, Mhuri yekwa Gwese, Chiweshe, recorded music that was played on African broadcasting channels for African services, but still the popularity of mbira remained limited.

The protest chants, and laments, in the rendition of Nhemamusasa by Ambuya Beauler Dyoko, ties in well with those expressed in the Negro spirituals.

I have lived as a missionary among African American in the West Coast of America for over twenty years. Coming from a journalistic background, I was curious to find out if there are still any similarities between Africans in the diaspora in America, and continental Africans. I have been fortunate enough to work with inner city communities, homeless, and low income, mostly immigrant families. It is at such levels where you observe people in their habitat, where you can observe people as they interact. As an African, I have been amazed by the similarities in the use of language between African American and continental Africans. The power of language is a tool that black people have used for communicating at different levels for centuries. Not only for survival, but African philosophy is encapsulated in the power of language, and its application. This power of language is employed in the composition of music, everyday speech, as well as witty slang. There is originality about the behavior of some African Americans, that you find commonly among rural communities of Africa. I witnessed this in most inner-city communities. As a person who did most of my practice of journalism in rural Africa, I have felt at home in the African American communities that I have worked in. Consequently, I am not surprised that the connections between Africans in the diaspora, and those on the continent express themselves in music, dance, food, relational dynamics. Listening to Nhemamusasa renditions, and Negro spirituals, one gets the same themes, expressed in different languages, as well as geographical locations. The songs have a message for someone. The singer is speaking to power in coded language, so that those in the fight against those in power understand the message. The themes of both Nhemamusasa, and Negro spirituals can unite together to reveal that in African culture, you do not confront those in power because it can backlash. However, you can have words that are explicit about the intended target of the message. The issue of confronting or speaking to power has not been received with kindness by most African governments in the post-colonial era because calls by civil society for democracy, and accountability are packaged in an un-African manner, and the Negro spirituals, and the Nhemamusasa genre give a glimpse of how those in power were addressed to avoid backlash. The songs reveal a relational dynamic between those who wield power, and those who are ruled. These are not the only similarities; there are many areas where you can witness the African qualities being expressed in elegant ways on both sides of the pond, that go beyond just genetic similarities. Of course, centuries of separation are bound to have ushered in other dynamics that are typical in any migration.

# Chapter 11

## Impact of abductions of Shona women

*Kuroora roora ndaroora nguruve,*

*Hanzvadzi yamai vako zvaisingarime*

*Kuroora roora ndaroora humba ini yamai vako*

*Hanzvadzi yamai vako zvaisingarime*

It is also important to realize that at the time when Nhemamusasa was performed, there were many Shona women who had been abducted and forced to march to Matabeleland or co -opted into Mfecane groups that wanted to replenish their ranks while in transit from South Africa in the northward excursion, Gwenyambira, in typical fashion of social commentator, presents a husband lamenting the quality of the wife that he married- *Kuroora, roora ndaroora nguruve (Although I have married, the wife is as filthy as a pig)*. The statement may seem like misplacement in a song but it is part of the whole lamentation of a plundered people. Their good women are all gone and they have to marry the ones not wanted by raiders. In this case, the woman in the verse has poor hygiene. This statement is a departure from the usual Shona tradition of addressing domestic complaints. Such intimate issues or conflicts were never fodder for public consumption. There were family members who mentored all relationships in a family, especially marriage. This extended family set up of mentoring and counseling married couples is a stark contrast to Gwenyambira's lamentation. The issue *Kuroora roora ndaroora nguruve,* is an expression of a broader issue in the Shona community where women en masse had been taken away by armed men and only the weak were left. The singer through Ambuya Beauler is mourning the abduction of Shona women by Ndebele soldiers. This is a societal dilemma that cannot be handled by individual families because the whole community is feeling the grief and loss of the daughters who had been abducted as well as their livestock. Chiwoniso carries the same message but using a specific dialect, Korekore.

*Nhemamusasa*

*Nhemamusasa*

*Wakaringe zuva iwe nhamo ichauya iwe*

*Iwe Nhemamusasa*

*Nhemamusasa*

*Wakaringe zuva nhamo ichauya*

*Pereka, Pereka, Pereka,*

*Pereka, pereka, pereka, pereka mvura mukaranga iwe*

92

*Pereka, Pereka, Pereka,*

*Pereka, pereka, pereka, pereka mvura mukaranga iwe*

Chiwoniso's rendition ties in with Ambuya Beauler's in both form and verse in terms of Mahon'era, emphasis and employment of euphemism. Both renditions have the same message but performed or expressed in a celebration for Chiwoniso and marriage woes and a political lament that ends up with an interaction with the Shona spirits by Ambuya Beauler. Chiwoniso's rendition starts with a warning to Nhemamusasa in an emphatic manner expressed in intonations. There are variations of pitch, in the mention of the name Nhemamusasa, as a way of driving the point home, in a bid to get attention from the listener of what is going to be said next. What is the point in this case? The following line brings it out. *Wakaringe zuva nhamo ichauya iwe- Do not be carried away watching the sun because danger is lurking. The same statement can be translated as: Do not observe the sun with reckless abandon because poverty is lurking.* According to Gwenyambira, Nhemamusasa is in a state where he watches the sun, as an expression of no worry about his life. Again, the dual if not multiple meanings are meant to convey a serious message through the employment of familiar terms in order to confuse the adversary while sending warning signals to possible victims. Nhemamusasa is warned not to relax because in real life Mfecane raids were sudden and devastating on unarmed villagers. Only the Shonas would get the cues being given by the *gwenyambira*. Emphasis is also made by Chiwoniso when she singles out Nhemamusasa, with a combination of a pronoun, and noun following each other *Iwe Nhemamusasa- You, Nhemamusasa. Iwe* is a second person pronoun used to take the role of the listener. As stated above, it helps with emphasizing the point being made in the warning to Nhemamusasa.

The sense of danger in the Shona environment is such that the simple pleasures of life, like children watching the sun, are hard to enjoy - *Wakaringe zuva iwe nhamo ichauya iwe.* There is an undertone in the song that Nhemamusasa is naïve. That is to be expected under normal circumstances, that children are naïve at some point in their growth cycle. However, a dangerous environment deprives children from going through the normal growth cycles because of fight or flight reactions to their environment. In psychology, when a person is faced with danger, they either respond instinctively in two ways; they fight or they flee. The fight or flight mode of existence does not allow children to be children. So, Nhemamusasa is true to form. He is a child watching the sun, and is oblivious to the reality of the insecurity that characterizes his environment at that particular point in time. The presence of conflict in any environment always affects the vulnerable who are children and women. The Nhemamusasa rendition by Chiwoniso brings that to the fore. The children in the community have to be in survival mode whether it is about death or dearth.

## Chapter 12

### The gender focus of Nhemamusasa

Nhemamusasa shows the attitude of Shona society towards women in the era of Mfecane. The Nhemamusasa genre was employed to express a season of trauma among the Shona. There are no names mentioned but the renditions largely relate to women. This signifies the value of and role that women played in Shona society especially in the face of the realities of abduction by different groups moving northwards from present day South Africa, who were escaping from the rule of Shaka, or were in the process of migration to other parts of Africa like Zwangendaba Gumbi Jele, and the Jere people, who are believed to have destroyed many of the structures at Great Zimbabwe, as they passed through. These different groups abducted locals whether women or men, in order to strengthen their military ranks, and for marriage purposes. There are indirect references to women made in both renditions which signify what the subject matter is all about women. Notwithstanding, the Shona belief that talking about women can be viewed as a sign of weakness makes it hard for the Gwenyambira to vocalize the issue at hand because in spite of the pain and sorrow, women should be seen in relation to the men.

Both renditions put women on a pedestal for a reason. This endearment of the Shona women by their men put them through another dark phase when at the turn of the twentieth century colonists struggled to get Shona men to leave their wives and seek gainful employment. There was no understanding by colonialists of the pain that Shona men had experienced at the hands of Mfecane raiders in which there was a lot of plundering by invading groups whether local or foreign. Women being weaker vessels, as well as keepers of homes could have been more vulnerable than their men, especially if they had to leave children behind when they were abducted in a bid to protect their wives, Shona men could not be away from home for long periods. No one related the behavior of the Shona men to the trauma caused by Mfecane raids which had instilled fear among Shona men of leaving their women in search of work in new settlements. As a result, assumptions were made that the Shona people were lazy and that they were controlled by their women who were viewed as having control over their men through sex. Yet, the fear of leaving their wives among the Shona was a reality based on experience and not because their wives had an insatiable sexual appetite which they used to control their men, but there were deep seated fears based on previous experiences among Shona people. Nhemamusasa, in its lyrics, gives a glimpse of the origin of the fear of the Shona men to leave their families in order to work in the mines and farms. Elizabeth Schmidt (1992) points out that Shona women were viewed as people of low moral standards who controlled their men through sex to the extent that they could not work on the farms because they wanted to be home to satisfy the sexual demands of their wives. What colonial settlers did not realize was the Shona society had been traumatized by the effects of Mfecane before the advent of the Pioneer column in 1890. When Shona men could not stay for too long away from their wives, the settler government blamed it on the sexual powers of Shona women. As a result of biased conclusions of the Shona people's attitudes towards employment in farms, and mines, by the settler government, laws were enacted and systems of control put in place to weaken the ability of Shona women to lead in church and in traditional structures. This systematic disempowerment of women still has some of its structures in place. This planned disenfranchisement that ties church, government and family structures is a major hurdle that the Shona woman is faced with in her quest to make her voice heard in meaningful ways. Nhemamusasa, lays the groundwork for the understanding of historical events and the evolution of the social history of the status of Shona women.

In Nhemamusasa, a Shona traditional song, depicts a woman in many relationships that make up her world. It is like every aspect of family relational dynamics connects to the woman in one way or another. It is the quality of these relational dynamics that reflect on whether a woman was weak or strong as viewed by the Shona society. The woman in Nhemamusasa is depicted prominently in these relational dynamics of mother, sister, wife, bride, and filthy daughter in law without mentioning her name in both renditions.

People of various nationalities have always praised the Shona people for their hospitality and humor even in the face of loss and pain. This reverberates in Chiwoniso's rendition which can be called the last part of a marriage ceremony. In spite of the trauma expressed in the prevailing social issues, the positive aspects of marriage ceremonies lighten the hard moments as the celebrations of a new union and the hope for a brighter future through the prospects of the birth of children lighten the moments. Chiwoniso urges the bride-*mukaranga* to serve the family that she has married into, persuasively. The atmosphere is a celebration that all hope is not lost in the abductions because marriage ceremonies are still being celebrated. However, it is clear that the focus of celebration is the bride and not the young man who has married her. This is deliberate in Chiwoniso's rendition because the woman' worth has been elevated as she is surrounded by possibilities of being abducted and taken to a land where she will never be seen. It is the woman who has become an endangered being and not the man. Granted, the men are equally endangered but women have become a scarce commodity on the marriage market. Consequently, those who can have a bride in the family put her on a pedestal to show her worth and not who she is as an individual. She is encouraged to serve the new family in a non-adversarial manner - *pereka, pereka, pereka mukaranga.*

# Chapter 13

## The beleaguered woman motif

**Motif in literature**, is a symbolic image or idea that appears frequently in a story. Motifs strengthen a story by adding images and ideas to the theme present throughout the narrative. In the Nhemamusasa renditions of the two artists, the woman does not vocalize her condition, as everything is done for her by Gwenyambira who gives her a voice throughout the song. In other words, the voice of a woman in Shona society is expressed through others. In doing so, Gwenyambira fulfills the role of social commentator. The woman is seen and not heard. Whether there is a sacredness or contempt is best known to Gwenyambira. However, the element of empathy for the condition of the woman reverberates throughout the renditions of Nhemamusasa- *hanzvadzi yamai vako zvaisingarime*. Instead of addressing her directly, Gwenyambira chooses to do so through her son. Perhaps, the purpose is to ease the pain that comes with directly confronting the woman. Is Gwenyambira being hypocritical in using this approach to point out a family problem. Not necessarily. Gwenyambira is conforming to the traditional Shona practice of addressing a problem in a roundabout way, so that the message is not harsh on the recipient. Assuming Nhemamusasa is a man, as indicated by the nature of chores that are mentioned- *roverera museve, hanzvadzi yamai vako zvaisingarime,* then the son is a recognized person who can represent his mother on family matters. In this case then, the mother is a minor who needs male figures to speak on her behalf. Where is the woman in it all? Why is she seen and not heard? She is in a beleaguered state- her brother cannot support her- *hanzvadzi yamai vako zvaisingarime*, the husband is lamenting that she is filthy- *ndaroora nguruve,* and the lurking danger may not spare the woman either- *wakaringe zuva nhamo ichauya*. The woman is seen in relations to others in the following relationships:

## 1. The woman as a bride

In both renditions of Nhemamusasa, the women are mentioned in relation to a man, though they are the main characters behind the song. Chiwoniso presents a newlywed or bride at a Shona family ceremony. She is somebody's wife.

*Pereka, Pereka Pereka*

*Pereka, Pereka, Pereka, Pereka Pereka mvura mukaranga iwe*

*Pereka, Pereka*

*Pereka, Pereka, Pereka, Pereka mvura mukaranga iwe*

Although the bride is being celebrated as she takes her new role as part of her husband's family, she is viewed through her relationship to her husband. The tone to urge the newly wed to fulfill the process of her integration into the new family seems to project circumstances that are not overtly enunciated. The singer packs the whole message in the word *pereka* said many times over. This can be open to many explanations. It was a common practice for Shona brides to perform this ritual at the time of marriage. Gwenyambira however seems to be emphatic on the process as if the whole process has taken on a new meaning. This may not be a reference to one bride but to the marriage process, that it has to be continued regardless of the prevailing circumstances. Hence the repeated use of *pereka* and *iwe- you-* to draw the attention of the person being addressed. *Mukaranga- bride* is not only being called upon to fulfill a ritual but that she should be aware that the process of marriage centers on her and as such she has a duty to be diligent in executing this role or else it loses meaning without her. If this is acceptable as valid speculation, then a Shona woman is playing a key role in the sustenance of the marriage institution even in her subservience, as she presents water to her new family. She is a reminder that in spite of the predicaments in the Shona society, the institution of marriage remains strong and the bride- *mukaranga* demonstrates this strength by courageously playing that role with the encouragement of her community.

The emphasis may be to point out the existence of a conflict within the world of the bride. This would not be due to opposition from in laws which has become commonplace in the new millennium because marriage was a major milestone in the old world. There is a sense of Gwenyambira urging Mukaranga to get the message of how important her move to join the new family is and the worth of the bridal rites of passage. Gwenyambira gives away a lot of information in the arrangement of the verses so that the audience understands that marriage was not easy during the time of Nhemamusasa as a character or as a genre of music.

The Shona society is fighting to keep its societal pillars standing due to calamities that affect the core of its existence which is marriage. Without being public about the sorrow of the Shona people, Gwenyambira has raised an alarm that the woman needs all the support for the Shona society to continue in strength. This could be the beginning of the customs that emphasize the protection of women of child bearing age, many of which persist in our time and regard women as objects of endearment and protection to the point of controlling whatever they do.

## 2. The woman as a mother and sister

Chiwoniso is emphatic about the message that follows the mention of the name Nhemamusasa repeatedly

*Iwe Nhemamusasa*

*Nhemamusasa Nhemamusasa Nhemamusasa*

*Nhemamusasa*

*Nhemamusasa Nhemamusasa Nhemamusasa*

Repetition plays the role of drawing attention to the listener who in this case is Nhemamusasa and the audience listening to Gwenyambira. Both Nhemamusasa and the audience have to prepare for the message that is to follow the repeated calling of Nhemamusasa's name. The message that is coming is very serious that the intended listener has to prepare to listen and do something about what is said.

The use of the second person pronoun *'Iwe'- You*, is also for the purposes of identifying the target listener so that no one is left wondering who the message is for and saying wake up! or please listen! After the listener is identified, yodeling is used to prepare the listener for the message that is coming. This is because apart from entertaining, Gwenyambira has a life changing message that is didactic, and the listener has to get it. As Gwenyambira realizes that the audience's attention is drawn to him or her, then yodeling is employed, intermittently with the intended message. The message is that Hanzvadzi yamai vako zvaisingarime. The woman is still the center of the Gwenyambira message but she is always highlighted in terms of her relationship to others. This comes from the belief that a woman is a system that sustains all the other aspects of life like Mother Earth, and as such she cannot stand as an entity but always as a part of something because who she is nourishes other systems; she has nothing of her own but she owns everything. Whether Gwenyambira is thinking in this manner is something open to one's perception of underlying issues being brought to the fore in the song.

Again, the woman is viewed in relation to her motherhood and then as a dependent sister, whose brother is referred to as one who does not till the land for a living- lazy.

*Haiya, horendende iye-iye*

*Hanzvadzi yamai vako zvaisingarime iwe*

*Haiwa, horendendeieye-iye*

*Hanzvadzi yamai vako zvaisingarime iwe*

*Iye horendende iyewi here ndende*

*Hanzvadzi yamai vako zvaisingarime iwe*

*Haiwa horendende iye*

*Hanzvadzi yamai vako  zvaisingarime*

## 3. The woman and Motherhood

By virtue of the minor status of women, it is understandable that Nhemamusasa is male. He is born to a woman who is a system that sustains other systems but that system needs support in turn. Just like in conservation where the catchment area is the origin of many river systems which then flow through many types of terrain, and support agriculture and industry, until it connects with other

107

rivers or empties itself into the ocean. For that system to be sustained the catchment has to be conserved so that all the other systems will not be sabotaged by the siltation of rivers. In the same manner, the woman who brings life into the earth and takes care of the family in all its extended forms needs to be 'conserved' in order for her to keep other systems functioning. Unfortunately, this is not the case for Nhemamusasa where dysfunction has set in through laziness if we pursue the literal meaning presented. Looking at a woman in relation to her environment may not be gender bias per se but an understanding that a system that nourishes many tentacles like a catchment of a river system is very fragile in itself if the necessary conservation measures are not rendered. Gwenyambira calls on Nhemamusasa to pay attention to the problem with his support system because his mother does not have a sustainable backup from a traditional pillar that should make her strong as a system, and this directly impacts Nhemamusasa. Nhemamusasa's mother has a lazy brother, who can neither mentor the nephew, nor be a strong voice on behalf of his sister as well as render material support. Consequently, Gwenyambira employs a variety of styles like yodeling/ magure, repetition, and pronouns to emphasize the message being conveyed to the recipient.

## 4. Woman as a sister to a brother

Intermittent yodeling and the central message, *Hanzvadzi yamai vako zvaisingarime iwe*, are employed in the song. Gwenyambira wants the audience to focus on the theme statement; *Hanzvadzi yamai vako zvaisingarime iwe*. Gwenyambira is inviting the audience to think deeper than just what they hear. What do they perceive after the same statement is repeated? There is something unusual about the mother's brother that Gwenyambira is driving home. Can it be just a message of laziness? How many lazy people are in the community? In literary terms, a woman who has brothers who are lazy is beleaguered because no one will stand up for her in defense with authority. By repeating the two lines over and over, Gwenyambira is begging the audience to think and then think again. It appears in this case the woman who is depicted as a sister has no support system for her to be able to sustain the systems that depend on her like Nhemamusasa, who would be her son in this case. The call is for those who are young and in need of support to rise up and fill a gap that has been created by the absence of support from the uncle. The uncle may not be practicing the traditional role of farming in order to produce food because he has been recruited into the ranks of the Dumbuseya or other Nguni warrior groups. Whichever way, Gwenyambira is saying that there is a social void created in the Shona community and unless the younger generation rises to fill up the gap, the support systems of the Shona society remain exposed to danger. So, is the mother a physical being or a system that is endangered by external forces, especially with Mfecane raids looming? Gwenyambira is inviting Nhemamusasa to think deeper and that call extends to any of the audience listening to the song because society is bereft of peace due to threats of one kind or another and hope is placed on the younger generation to rise up and do something about it- *Usaringe zuva nhamo ichauya iwe- do not watch the sun because poverty is pending- Do not be idle.*

In both Chiwoniso and Ambuya Beauler renditions, the woman's worth is seen through her brother, her bridal rites of passage- *mukaranga.* There is an aura of divinity of this woman who has no name but who she is, is expressed through her roles and relationships.

Mbuya Beauler Dyoko reinforces what Chiwoniso renders in her version by introducing a weapon of war and hunting before she raises the issue of *Hanzvadzi yamai vako zvaisingarime.* Dyoko takes the issue of the woman as a broken system by focusing on her weaknesses as seen by her spouse; *Kuroora roora ndaroora nguruve*

*Roverera museve*

*Hanzvadzi yamai vako zvaisingarime*

*Roverera museve*


*Kuroora roora ndaroora nguruve,*

*Hanzvadzi yamai vako zvaisingarime*

*Hiya woye woyere ona*

*Hanzvadzi yamai vako zvaisingarime*


*Kuroora ndaroora nguruve*

*Hanzvadzi yamai vako zvaisingarime*

*Iya*

 *woiye*

*worende heya*

    *The statement kuroora, ndaroora nguruve,* could also mean that the man married an undesirable woman. This may sound rather far-fetched but when one understands that Nguni, and Dumbuseya soldiers abducted fair skinned women mostly, according to oral history narrations, leaving the darker skinned ones, then Shona men were left with no choice but to marry the women of darker skin tone. Not that there's anything wrong with a dark-skinned woman, but abductions limited the choice that Shona men could have among their own people. While in advanced societies with many racial groupings including those of African descent, colorism is a major issue, we see its primitive expression in the Nguni- Shona relations before 1900. However, in this case, the lighter brighter skin tone was a liability for Shona girls, who became prime targets during raids. **Colorism** is prejudice or discrimination against individuals with a dark skin tone, typically among people of the same ethnic or racial group. Oral history disseminated at drinking parties described the brutality of Nguni raids at the height of the kingdom of Bulawayo. Of course, that information became commonplace in the villages as some abducted villagers made their way home when Bulawayo fell to the British South Africa Company. The survivors, some of whom lived until the 1970s, described how lighter skinned women were given to the ruling class of the Nguni, and comprised most of the female abductees. Some villagers recounted how the raids were carried out. The Ndebeles or Dumbuseya would hide themselves but one of them skilled in making sounds would cry like an abandoned baby. This appealed to the instincts of women who would try to locate the crying baby. Suddenly, the women found themselves among the raiders. In Ambuya Beauler Dyoko, Gwenyambira is expressing anger that though he has fulfilled the traditional custom of marrying a wife, he is not happy about having her. However, Gwenyambira had to carefully craft the words because if the raiding groups got to know of such sentiments, then there could be a serious backlash. Still Gwenyambira says something about the issue, thereby fulfilling the role of social commentator.

## Chapter 14

### Nhemamusasa and the treatment of Shona women by missionaries in the early days of colonialists

The Shona woman regained prominence during the early days of colonialism for negative reasons. Without any appreciation of the effects of Mfecane on Shona people both missionaries and the colonial administrators' heaped accusations on an already ravaged gender. As a result, measures were taken to curb the strength of the Shona woman through the church and society in general, thereby putting the death knell on her chances to recover from trauma and regain self-worth.   Schmidt (1992) explores the plight of Shona women between 1870 and 1939. Shona women were blamed for everything that happened in the colonial settlement of Rhodesia. They were described as lazy, slothful, immoral, frivolous, savagely and uncivilized.

For instance, Father Richartz, a Jesuit, the Superior of Chishawasha described Shona girls as "...devoid of seriousness both of mind and character" He may have been correctly describing traumatized women, although he may not have cared to explore the reasons behind the behavior. From such beliefs among Jesuits was born a decision not to employ Shona women as teachers and catechists because 'it would jeopardize the whole mission work because the women's characters were deemed unfit for any serious occupation.

In the church, only white women were allowed to lead Ruwadzano as senior leadership. This was carefully designed to ensure that white women, who felt threatened by the sexual potency of black women, controlled them in the church and opposed their gainful employment.

There were always exceptions to the rule by oppression, as individuals like Native Commissioner Posselt who called for the improvement of the status of Shona women, were criticized by the church and other administrators. He had been touched by the plight of elderly women who became destitute when their husbands refused to pay Hut Tax for them.

Colonial administrators blamed Shona women for the shortages of labor that they experienced. So, they enacted laws like The Native Adultery Punishment Ordinance in 1916. This was because African women were blamed for adultery, venereal diseases, and unhygienic conditions at home as well as their sex drives that gave them control over men. Man would not go to work, choosing rather to stay at home in order to satisfy the sex drives of their wives. Even the African mothers were blamed for protecting their children from working under difficult conditions in the mines. The African mothers would ask their husbands to sell cattle to raise money for Hut Taxes for their adult sons.

This period is preceded by Nhemamusasa when Bulawayo, and other Nguni groups flourished in the area north of Limpopo River, strengthened by the raids and abduction of women. Other indigenous groups like the Dumbuseya who were part of the Shonas had learned Nguni style raids, as well as fighting techniques when they were incorporated into the ranks of the newcomers. They abducted women and pillaged many communities, to the extent that it became difficult to correctly identify the raiders, so they were collectively called Ndebeles.

After 1890, there was still no reprieve for Shona women because their efforts to protect the family unit were interpreted wrongly by the colonial administrators. The efforts by Shona men to be there for their wives in order to protect them from possible raids were viewed as some form of control of the men by their women through sex. It is possible that Shona people were not aware at grassroots levels that the Nguni raids were no longer a threat after the fall of Bulawayo. They still wanted to protect their families by being physically present. The experiences before 1890 had been traumatic enough to induce fear among Shona people of foreigners and the colonialists were no exception. This is not to say that Shona interaction with foreigners were a new phenomenon, because they had been trading with the Portuguese, and other groups before, but the Mfecane period was characterized by raids and abductions, which obviously induced fear among many Shona communities.

However, the misunderstanding of the plight of Shona people caused the women to sink deeper into an inferior status because the settler government supported a domestic setting where women were oppressed by their husbands as a way of systematically establishing control over them. The song Nhemamusasa helps to shed some light on the dynamics of relations that brought one plight of Shona women after another at the hands of Mfecane raiders, colonialists and missionaries.

## Chapter 15

## Rain making ceremonies- *Mitoro*

The Mbira genre of music goes beyond just entertainment as mbira is an instrument that is sometimes accompanied by songs that are used for traditional rites among the Shona especially for rainmaking and evoking the spirits of the dead at traditional dances called *bira- singular, mapira- plural*

These are ceremonies designed to appease the rain making deities of the land in order to have abundant harvests that last from one season to another. These ceremonies are usually presided over by traditional leaders and the elderly. Participation is limited to women who are post-menopausal as well and girls who have not yet reached puberty. Rain making ceremonies are usually held near water bodies and or in mountains or caves. Although the people who actively participate in the ceremony are given specialized roles, the rest of the community contributes the grains and other items used in the ceremony because the whole community benefits from abundant harvests. The ceremonies are held in a hierarchical manner from the local community, to regional level and then to the national level where the ruling spirit is appeased through libations and the playing of the mbira and dance. Spirit mediums which are regional representatives of the national deity called mhondoro preside over such ceremonies. The use of the mbira for traditional ceremonies does not strip it of its relevance as an instrument that is played for entertainment. Like in ngano, mbira music is also employed to put across messages that may be deemed as hard to confront a person with. As a result, correction is made through the choice of words employed in the song. This is why there are variations of Nhemamusasa where the singer or mushauri can employ words that suit the circumstances. For instance, Stella Chiweshe presents a rendition of Nhemamusasa related to a time of famine. *Makasara muri vangani nzara? Kana makasara muri vanomwe…pasi kwenyika ndoinda newe maroro.- How many of you have survived famine? If there are seven of you, I will take you to the underworld where there is food in the form of maroro- a traditional fruit.* This does not change the original song but the desire to relay a message causes mushauri to throw in words that address some social ills or any other message. One does not just take on the role of *mushauri,* they have to be a person who thinks fast in order to make sure that the blend of the words and the music are seamless. One can also argue that while the role of musicians and artists is to educate, entertain and inform, Nhemamusasa could have started off like an ordinary pass time mbira song but later evolved into a ceremonial song for *bira or mitoro- rain making ceremonies.* The fact that women participate in playing mbira means at one-point communities gathered to celebrate the harvests together and there was no segregation over who should play the instrument or not.

In her rendition of Nhemamusasa Ambuya Beauler Dyoko brings in the element of speaking to spirits who are attracted by the playing of mbira - *Ndanzwa ngoma kurira- I heard the sound of music.* The mbira is referred to as a drum- ngoma, which is another Shona way of using a collective term in reference to music instruments.

Ambuya Dyoko introduces the arrival of spirits by saluting them as Changamire- a title for a ruler. In other words, the playing of mbira attracts ruling spirits, which the living is subject to. Although Dyoko salutes the arrival of Changamire, or the esteemed spirit, which is likely to be accompanied by lesser ones, there is a request for permission by spirits to access the realm of the living. If living beings do not open the door to the spirits of the dead, then they cannot come into that realm, regardless of their rank. This is a spiritual law. It is expressed in terms of human possession by spirits, which only do so with the permission of the individual or some senior family member, who has authority over a family. The same rule applies at the point of death. When a person is dying, or before they die, they usually have dreams of being embraced by dead relatives. Sometimes, a person on a sick bed tells those around them that they are being called by dead members of their family. This is a spiritual order that is operational between the living and the dead, and one cannot just cross into the other's territory. It is a law of God that governs the cosmos.

The repetition of the word Changamire, signifies the honor being accorded to the spirits that have arrived, under the leadership of a strongman.

*Hani Changamire, Changamire*

*Changamire*

*Changamire*

*Changamire*

*Changamire*

Tikinya is also repeated to describe the motion of the strongman. It is a grand appearance of authority, and Dyoko feels it and acknowledges.


*Tikinya*

*Tikinya*

*Tikinya*

*Tikinya*

*Tikinya*

*Tikinya*

*Tikinya*

*Tikinya*

*Tikinya*

*Tikinya*

Ambuya Beauler  Dyoko, also goes further to describe the motion of the spirits, as she sees them as they arrive to the sound of mbira playing. *Apo, apo, apo- There, there, there,* as she notices spirits in numbers approaching the venue. In this case the playing of mbira becomes a convergence of the living and the spirits of the dead.

*Apo, apo, apo*

*Apo, apo, apo*

*Apo, apo, apo*

*Apo, apo, apo,*

*Apo, apo, apo*

*Apo, apo, apo*

*Hani*

Ambuya Beauler Dyoko delves further into the conversation between Gwenyambira and spirits by presenting it in song, making the atmosphere lively with interactions at human and spiritual levels. The spirits salute Ambuya Beauler Dyoko and her singing partner Cosmas- *Tanzwa ngoma kurira Beauler.*

*Tanzwa ngoma kurira Cosmas. We had the sound of the drum Beauler.*

*We heard the sound of the drum Cosmas.*

Then the spirits beg to be accepted into the performance, as they say *"Kana uchitida tinogara pano"- If you welcome us, we will stay*

*Even the way that Ambuya Beauler Dyoko announces the*

*arrival of the spirit, she says Tikinya, Tikinya*

## Chapter 16

## Nhemamusasa is part of Old-World Shona Romance

There are variations of the song denoting the different times or situations in which it was sung. As mentioned earlier, Nhemamusasa fits into the world of pre-colonial Shona romance. It explores the relationship of nature and the people living on it. People depend on hunting and agriculture as well as securing their survival through military training so that they can ward off invaders. When you listen to the rendition by Ambuya Beauler Dyoko, as she plays and sings you, immediately pick up the war and hunting vibes to Nhemamusasa as she says: *Roverera museve, hanzvadzi yaamai vako zvaisingarime roverera museve…* That is not all; you also get the relational dynamics of a thriving community. Mbuya Beauler Dyoko encapsulates all these feelings as Gwenyambira or Mushauri status. She brings an old world to the new through a summation of broad and serious issues in the Shona culture. Issues that may have been at the center of existence which over time paled out as society became more dynamic and sophisticated. In rendering Nhemamusasa in such a somber blend of the thumb piano and lyrics, Ambuya Beauler Dyoko is saying that the core of the Shona culture has not changed because people are still moved by that which was initiated centuries before their birth. In other words, the Shona people of today are still much the same as those of yesteryear; only their faces have changed and their environment has been tamed more than it was in the past but core issues have not changed. This suggests the resilience of a community in that they have welcomed interactions with outsiders and benefited in many ways in such relationships but the core of who they are has not been changed.

The lyrics suggest a military setting where a younger person is taught how to fight in order to subsist as a soldier because he does not come from a family that makes a livelihood from agriculture. *Roverera* is an adverb used to urge the cadet or recruit to learn the skills of using a spear- *Roverera museve*. This is not surprising since elders in the Shona communities had to teach the younger generation the skills necessary to survive and eventually take over the leadership of the family and community. Gwenyambira is expressing the mood in a training camp for a cadet who is learning the art of using a spear in battle. One gets the impression that the trainee or cadet has nothing else to hold on to except developing the use of the spear. *Roverera Museve* – stabs the victim with force or strike the nerve that will take your enemy out in a fight. This implies that the person receiving the instruction is an armature.

In the *Chizukuru* register of the Shona culture, a grandchild of a family plays a major role in the relational dynamics of a family. This is more so if the grandchild is a man. The man child born to a daughter of a family has a voice that is respected in his mother's family as well as his father's. To his mother's family, he is looked upon as a security of the daughter in the family that she marries into because she brought forth an heir. The man child is an assurance of the continuity of the family name in any Shona family. It is important for both the mother's family and the fathers to equip a male child with skills, to lead, demonstrate wisdom at the courts among other men, make the right choice of a wife and raise children who are to carry the family name on and on. The Gwenyambira, in this case Ambuya Beauler Dyoko, is weaving these beliefs and practices in her rendition of Nhemamusasa. However, the lyrics carry an undertone of dysfunction which is affecting the younger generation- *Hanzvadzi yamai vako zvaisingarime – since your mother's brother does not till the land. In other words, since your uncle is lazy.*

**Hanzvadzi yamai vako zvaisingarime – since your mother's brother does not till the land- for a living. / Since your uncle is lazy.**

In Shona culture, individuals play varied important roles in a family, such as counseling and general upkeep of peace in a family and the community at large. Roles vary in importance depending on the type of relationship. Modeling good behavior by individuals who hold important positions in the family relational dynamics is viewed as integral to the upbringing of good citizens because charity begins at home.

Some of the important roles in a Shona family also have a register that they use in relaying some messages. For instance, a newly married wife who discovers that her husband is not handling her well sexually would not dare confront the husband. Instead, she wakes up early, as expected of her to prepare food and clean up but instead of doing her chores quietly, she sings loudly to break the silence of the morning. The elders of the family know that cue. They immediately call on the men in the family who are either a grandfather, or the uncle of the husband to address the problem. Sometimes, the lament of the bride is not news to the family because they may have been aware of their son's sexual challenges. This awareness of a young boy's sexual abilities is manifested at puberty, when those members of the family assigned to the role of helping the younger ones through the pathway to adulthood take young boys to the river where their semen is examined in order to ascertain virility. The women also train the girls on how to walk with a gait that attracts attention. The girls are made to carry pitchers of water and walk straight in a manner that allows their bodies to demonstrate their feminine features with a view to attract men. Many other things are done to and for the Shona boys and girls as a rite of passage to manhood or womanhood. If these roles are not available, then the upcoming generation may 'lack manners'- 'kushaya hunhu'.

When a bride cries out for help in song in the early hours of the morning, there are secret family meetings held among the elders both men and women, to solve the problem. If the issue of the man's virility is a known problem to the family, then arrangements are made, clandestinely to have the husband's brother have sex with the wife for the sake of her satisfaction as well as rearing the children for the impotent brother. This was supposed to be a top secret in the family which the elders take to their graves. That arrangement was kept a secret for two reasons; the one called upon to help out could be married and if the secret is known then his marriage might have problems too from his wife. The lawful husband could be jealous and start a long-lasting dispute with his brother who is asked to help the family stay together. This is an extended version of the biblical practice where a brother of a deceased man had sex with the widowed woman in order to raise a family for the dead so that their name would not be forgotten in ancient Israel. Such an arrangement is also a safeguard against the breeding of bastards in a family. The secrets that shrouded family dynamics meant that those assigned such responsibilities played a very important role in the life of a young person.

If we take the literary meaning of *Hanzvadzi yamai vako zvaisingarime*, we still see the aspect of mentoring of the younger generation by those who are older and more experienced, as we are presented with a dysfunctional dynamic in which a person who is supposed to be mentoring a younger person is not fulfilling that role, so someone else takes over to help out.

It is clear that an elderly soldier or hunter is training a protégé on hunting or skills of using a spear in battle and hunting. Ambuya Beauler Dyoko goes further to mention the circumstances of the young man who is faced with a broken support system- *hanzvadzi yamai vako zvaisingarime/ since your uncle is lazy.* In other words, one of the pillars of support for Nhemamusasa's life is broken and that means the young man has to find other sources of support in order to make it in life. Nhemamusasa has to have a skill in order to survive in his time. Unfortunately, becoming a soldier, hunter and farmer are the major preoccupations in the instance presented. Why is the uncle brought in by Ambuya Beauler Dyoko? This is because uncles played a major role in the development of their nieces and nephews. Not only that, in the world of Nhemamusasa, the strength of a woman was not exhibited in her physical attributes only, because she was regarded as a minor who needed men to stand up and speak on her behalf. The men were either her parents, brothers and uncles who made sure that she was backed up in case of marital problems or meeting her needs during a famine if she was married to a poor man. If this support system was weak, then the woman had no protection and it was even worse for her children who would have no role models in the form of maternal uncles. As pointed out earlier, euphemism is employed to hide the actual purpose of the statement hanzvadzi *yamai vako zvaisingarime* in the Nhemamusasa genre. The likely reason for doing so being the fear of confronting the problem of Shona people abduction by Mfecane raiding soldiers who were regarded as *vasingarime*-those who did not live on agriculture- lazy.

The definitions of roles have been confined to the ones relevant to the text under scrutiny.

## Chapter 17

### Identity markers and poetic devices used in Nhemamusasa

It is important to understand why the variations of the Zezuru dialects are employed in Nhemamusasa. Korekore, in particular with words like Pereka, meaning to handover or give, may help explain why Gwenyambira from such a tribe would sing a piece like Nhemamusasa. The Zezuru dialect mainly incorporates Korekore, and Budya, which were spoken in areas far away from Bulawayo.

To this day, these areas of Zimbabwe which are in the Mashonaland region have not had as much Ndebele cultural influence as most of the southern regions which were quickly assimilated into the Ndebele system of government, by virtue of their proximity to Zululand were former impis of Shaka Zulu ailed from.. However, there were strong dynasties like those of Matsveru who led the House of Chivi, during the height of Mfecane, who succeeded in resisting Ndebele hegemony in the Nyaningwe hills battle. Ndebele authority did not have much influence in Chivi, but there were the Dumbuseya group which was composed of both Nguni and locals who effected Ndebele style raids in what is Midlands province today.

Nhemamusasa is a Zezuru outcry over the disruption of life by the raiders who could have included the assimilated Shona people from southern regions. The song decries the destruction of pillars of Zezuru identity, which were marriage, farming, celebrations and worship of ancestors. Therefore, the song is a pitch by Gwenyambira to call on the locals to fight for the preservation of the foundations of their identity which was facing a threat of possible erosion through incessant raids.

There is a distinct Korekore dialect describing the bridal welcome ceremony – *pereka, pereka- give, give or handover, handover.* The Nhemamusasa activity or song could have been borne in a deeply engrained Zezuru practices which were later adopted by other Shona subgroups. Even most mbira players, and groups come from Zezuru families that use mbira playing in entertainment, and ceremonies, notably Mhuri yekwaGwese, and female performers like Stella Chiweshe from the same bloodline.

Terms like *Mukaranga,* have evolved from meaning a young bride/wife to defining a group of Shona speaking people based in the southern regions of Zimbabwe. The term could have been reinforced as an identity marker during the early days of colonial occupation in which under the policy of divide and rule, people from one tribe were sent into another tribe to police it. Some tribes did not deal kindly with their fellow Africans, in enforcing the settler demands on local people resulting in rifts among ethnic groups, some of which persist to this day. In Chiwoniso's rendition, mukaranga is a newly married woman or bride.

## Mhururu- ululation

Ululation is commonly used among all Shona speaking groups. When Chiwoniso opens her rendition with a ululation, then it means that an atmosphere is one of celebration, and festivities

## Vocal styles

The vocal styles
are **mahon'era, kudeketera** and **huro**.

**Mahon'era** refers to the vocables, which are used across Shona dialects because they have their origin in the ngano/Folklore register, in which a story teller employs the technique in order to prepare the audience for what he or she is about to say, or to buy time as the storyteller thinks of what to say next because there is no text to follow in folk stories because most of them were traditionally used to correct a wrong that is ongoing through indirect confrontation.

*Hiya*

*Hiya hah*

Hoo- horendere hiya

Hiya

Hiya- hah

Hoo-horendere hiya

Hiya

Hiya wore e

Woo-horendere hiya

**Kudeketera** is poetic language, carefully employed to convey a message in a particular tone of humility designed to implore the one being addressed to hear and show compassion, usually a senior person or being. This is very common in prayer to ancestors, where Shona people pray to the dead who have the power to bless or curse a person. The one offering the prayers has to be conscious of this fact, hence the language has to be well thought out. This is not employed by Chiwoniso rendition because it is a celebration of a marriage ceremony. But in Nhemamusasa rendition by Ambuya Beauler Dyoko, there is a great deal of kudeketera, which takes on the version of receiving or welcoming spirits which can be referred to as higher powers because the term **Changamire** - king, is repeated as a form of obeisance, and acknowledgement of the presence of someone with a senior rank. Implying that in Shona culture, the spirits of the dead are viewed as having more authority like kings, deserving of honor. The excitement in Ambuya Beauler Dyoko when she sings about the arrival of spirits, welcoming them, Again, a sense of exhibition of diplomatic language in welcoming the kings from another world is expressed. There is a change of register from lamenting about a poor quality of marriage to an excited mood of a hospitable welcome characteristic of VaNyai- Diplomats.

*Hani Changamire, Changamire*

*Changamire*

*Changamire*

*Changamire*

*Changamire*

Again, the term Changamire in the past was commonly associated with dialects of Mashonaland-Zezuru, Korekore, and Budya. On the other hand, the Karanga dialect used the term **VaShe**- for king. This also is a demonstration that Nhemamusasa had a specific geographic influence in terms of its origin, performance and the message that it carried, as well as occasions on which it was performed. The regions of Mashonaland, commonly played mbira during rain making ceremonies and celebrations. The ceremonies were performed mostly by water bodies because the Shona people in general worship marine spirits Chigwedere (1980). Apart from acknowledging the presence of higher powers,

Ambuya Beauler Dyoko presents the spirits responding to the playing of mbira by saying, *Ndanzwa ngoma kurira- we heard the sound of music. In other words, the spirits have taste. They can hear the sound of music and be excited enough to respond.*

*Kana uchitida tinogara pano- If you want us here, we will stay-*

However, spirits have no bodies, so they are asking Gwenyambira for permission to mingle with the living. The spirits are not only attending the mbira playing ceremonies but if there happens to be people who are open to being possessed at such occasions, and then they become spirit mediums who are possessed by certain groups of spirits. This type of dynamic between the playing of instruments, and the attraction of spirits to the playing of certain instruments is not limited to mbira playing but can happen even at modern concerts. The issue is whether individuals in attendance can accept the request of the spirits to become mediums or not, or whether the people attending a concert and listening to beautiful music have an understanding that just as music appeals to the depths of their souls, spirits also experience the same effect. In the church, such an experience is called worship, which invokes the presence of the Holy Spirit, while in certain types of secular musical gatherings, there can be an invoking of the spirits of the dead.

In this case, the playing of mbira attracted spirits to join the mortals, who were also listening to Ambuya Beauler. This practice of attracting spirits through the playing of an instrument is also mentioned in the Bible, in which prophets called for the playing of instruments in order to invoke the Holy Spirit presence- 1 Samuel 16:23.

Perhaps the *Tikinya, tikinya, tikinya* could be Gwenyambira's imagination of the motion of spirits coming from their dwelling at the beckoning of the sound of music, to join the audience at the ceremony or event. Ambuya Beauler shifts from singing about the social challenges in her community as she salutes higher authorities among her audience- **Changamire- lord/ king.** The weight of the authorities present is expressed through the repetition of the term Changamire. In other words, Ambuya Dyoko is dealing with the natural realm as well as the spiritual, and she salutes the unseen spirits by acknowledging their elevated status. This is followed by Tikinya, a term that might describe the motion of the beings that shows their power. Usually, the living are the ones that present their petitions to spirits but in this case the spirits show up and Gwenyambira is the first to salute them.

*Apo, apo, apo,* appears to indicate the sudden appearance of spirits on the scene from everywhere,

such that wherever you look, you see them coming
with to the gathering, walking in their authority.

*Hani Changamire, Changamire*

*Changamire*

*Changamire*

*Changamire*

*Changamire*

*Tikinya*

*Tikinya*

*Tikinya*

*Tikinya*

*Tikinya*

*Tikinya*

*Tikinya*

*Tikinya*

*Tikinya*

*Tikinya*

*Apo, apo, apo*

*Apo, apo, apo*

*Apo, apo, apo*

*Apo, apo, apo,*

*Apo, apo, apo*

*Apo, apo, apo*

*Hani*

*Ndanzwa ngoma kurira*

*Kana uchitida togara pano*

*Maiwee*

    Again, Ambuya Beauler Dyoko does not depart from the ngano style as she mentions the names of the people present at the gathering including her name. She presents the audience as an interactive group that talks to the spirits, a common practice among Shona people. *Ndanzwa ngoma kurira Beauler, Ndanzwa ngoma kurira Cosmas.* In other words, mbira playing unites the living and the spirits. In this case the thumb piano then qualifies to be called an instrument of the ancestors in terms of the context in which Ambuya Dyoko presents it. However, this is towards the end of her performance, after she has sung about the matters that are of immediate concern to her community. Whether she preserves the best for last is not clear but what comes out clearly is that while Chiwoniso rendition is celebrating a marriage ceremony in the face of an unstable environment; Ambuya Beauler Dyoko ends her rendition with a celebration of the gathering of an audience that brings together spirits and human beings. There seems to be so much excitement with the arrival of spirits, that the pain of warfare (roverera museve) is swallowed up in the uniting of the living and dead at the sound of music.

*Maiwee*, is a term that expresses regret or sorrow. The same word in both sound and spelling can also be used to express the depth of fun, which is how it is used by Ambuya Beauler Dyoko. There is so much fun on the dance floor with Tikinya, tikinya, tikinya- a possible expression of a dance move. In the heat of the excitement, there is a cry to express the peak of the fun moment by shouting *Maiwee!*

Chiwoniso uses a different word to express the charged atmosphere due to the sound of music and mbira playing- *Iiiiwee- You*. The term sounds like a warning of disapproval but in fact Gwenyambira is saying *"You can't beat this"*. The **penultimate** syllables are employed by both artists to emphasize the high-level ecstasy- instead of just *Iwe- you*, there is need to emphasize that it's not just an address to another in the second person pronoun in Chiwoniso's rendition, but a beckoning to whoever is present at the dance floor to share in the joy. *Iwe*, has emphasis added to *I-i-i-iwe*! The penultimate strain is high pitched, in line with the mood obtained in the atmosphere charged by the playing of mbira.

*Ambuya Beauler Dyoko employs the penultimate lines in their verses. Maiwee!* Maiwe-e, can be an expression of pain, but in this case, it is a high-pitched emphatic expression of excitement. Presumably, this may be the excitement due to mbira played by Ambuya Beauler that also attracts and excites spirits of the dead to the point of asking to join the party. It's not only the audience, who are enjoying the mbira playing, but also gwenyambira, who doubles up to express pleasure on his or her own behalf as well as echoing the mood of the audience.

Penultimate is a Latin word which means "next to last" or "second to last." In *Iiiiwee, "i"and "e" syllables are added to a word "iwe"- "you"* to bring out the emphasis'

A **syllable is a unit** of pronunciation having one vowel sound, with or without surrounding consonants, forming the whole or a part of a word.

In Maiwee, "e" syllable is added to the last in order to convey the intended meaning.

## Idiophonic expressions

Ambuya Beauler Dyoko employs these expressions to describe what she senses or sees spiritually as the motion of high-ranking spirits visiting her mbira party. This may be her ultimate objective. To play mbira with skill to the point of drawing the attention of spirits. Such occasions are called *bira*- traditional gathering to appease familial spirits or at *mitoro* - rainmaking ceremonies where gatherings may be by sacred pools. In succeeding to draw the attention of the spirits of the dead, Ambuya Beauler Dyoko has achieved a high level of performance that is acknowledged by the spirits because not everyone is able to achieve that by simply playing mbira. It takes a certain level of skill, and understanding of some traditional rites to play mbira in a way that appeases *vadzimu- ancestral spirits*.

In typical style of someone used to interacting with vadzimu, Dyoko, salutes- *Hani, Changamire, Changamire*- King, King and then describes what she sees, as the spirits or spirit moves towards the gathering- *Tikinya, Tikinya*- a motion that sounds like the walking of someone with power, or the motion of a big being or animal. The employment of idiophonic expressions, could be an expression of a Gwenyambira who is overwhelmed by the sudden appearance of a spiritual being with authority, or an inability to describe the aura of the movement of a spirit that has authority, that Gwenyambira can only describe the motion. It is a sacred moment for Gwenyambira, but one that she has to share with the audience who may be eagerly waiting for her announcement of the arrival of the ancestors. Her salutation, Changamire, changes the atmosphere because someone with power has arrived, and all the dynamics of the playing and dance acknowledges this change.

To let the audience, know that it is not only the Changamire spirit that has come, she employs another set of idiophonic expressions, to alert the audience that there is more than one visitor. *Apo, Apo, Apo- there, there, there,* express that the spirits have not arrived in a single file but are spread over an area. This is important in that if the spirit that has come is a Changamire- King spirit, then its weight is expressed by the number of lesser spirits accompanying it as subjects. In other words, even in the spirit realm, those that wield power have followers, and servants. So, Ambuya Beauler Dyoko salutes the Changamire, because it is the one with authority, but the presence of other spirits is expressed with *Apo, Apo.* Make no mistake that the lesser spirits can speak in the presence of the chief spirit. In so doing they would be challenging the Changamire/King spirit. In this case, one has to assume that the one who says *Tanzwa ngoma kurira,* and *kana uchitida tinogara pano is the* Changamir*e spirit because it speaks on behalf of its followers.*

*Ndanzwa ngoma kurira Beauler*

*Kana uchitida togara pano*

*Maiwee*

*Ndanzwa ngoma kurira Cosmas*

*Kana uchitida togara pano*

*Maiwee...*

**Huro / yodeling.**

Excitement is further expressed through yodeling.

Yodeling (Huro) is a form of singing which involves repeated and rapid changes of pitch between the low-pitch and the high-pitch

In Ambuya Beauler Dyoko, yodeling is preceded by spirits introducing themselves and the reason why they are joining the mortals- it is because they heard the sound of the instrument. This is followed by yodeling which expresses more excitement. Gwenyambira ushers in the excitement, probably because the presence of spirits which Shona people believe in is a sign that all hope is not lost. Therefore, there is reason to cease from lamenting and take to the dance floor. Gwenyambira becomes the custodian of the atmosphere that prevails in any particular gathering because he or she knows the pain but also the times of merriment.

All the dialects of Shona employ yodeling to express joy in an atmosphere deemed as positive. One song that employs merriment through yodeling is *Yakarira Mucherechere,* often sung in the southern parts of Zimbabwe at the threshing floor as people gather for threshing small grains during harvest. The song does not say that there was abundant rain but it describes what the rain did, resulting in abundant harvests. *Mucherechere* is an idiophonic expression of the beauty of rain as it thunders and pours down. Nhunga Makore is also another term to describe rain in an endearing manner.

Chiwoniso yodels too in her rendition to express the joy and peak of excitement. In other words, while the song carries heavy messages of pain, Shona people always find a way to celebrate even in the face of pain. The idea is to dance away the pain and be optimistic about tomorrow, because life is for those who want to live and the living dance and rejoice.

Chiwoniso uses yodeling as well.

*Ayiyere Iye*

*Ayiyere iye*

*Aiyere iye*

*Ayire iye*

*Ayiyere iye*

*Aiyere iye*

*Ayi yere iye*

## Chapter 18

### Expressive language

From the styles employed by both artists in their renditions of Nhemamusasa, it is clear that the song has its roots in Shona folklore of being expressive, as demonstrated by its close relationship with Ngano as well as other patterns of Shona customs of marriage ceremonies, relational dynamics (*hanzvadzi yamai vako zvaisingarime*) employed to portray a message. The repetition of words and phrases to emphasize the most important messages is amply used throughout the two versions of the song. The words introducing the two renditions set the tone of what is following. Chiwoniso starts with an ululation, to mark a celebration at a marriage ceremony, but still draws the listener to other social ills going on in the Shona community, which have been examined earlier. Both artists employ language that demonstrates the peak of excitement among Shona people. Chiwoniso uses *Iiiiwee*! The expression only comes after the audience has been aroused by the pleasure derived from mbira playing, so it is not put at the beginning of the song because the audience is not yet warmed up. The *Iiiiwee* can sound like a confrontational expression by Gwenyambira but to the contrary, Gwenyambira interacts with an excited audience as a way of acknowledging their oneness in a moment of exhilaration.

Ambuya Beauler Dyoko, does the same by presenting a combative tone - *roverera museve*. Then a somewhat insulting response from the victim of attack to the one thrusting the arrow/ or assegai. Next comes the lament- *Kuroora, roora, ndaroora nguruve*- a man acknowledges marrying a wife with qualities of a pig. In other words, he is not happy with the pedigree that he has brought into his life and family. Once that message is communicated, there is a complete shift by Dyoko to an interaction with the spirit realm. Whether this is at a rainmaking ceremony or just a traditional worship meeting is differentiated by the mention of names of people in the audience, who are also interacting with spirits-

*Tanzwa ngoma kurira Beauler, Tanzwa ngoma kurira Cosmas.* Just like in folklore where songs are sung to address issues that are current, the mention of the people present at the gathering indicates the Gwenyambira role of social commentator; whether playing for pleasure or to invoke spirits. Ambuya Beauler brings out the notion that music is a universal language that both the living and the dead hear. When the living and the dead interact, there are pacts or agreements that are entered- *Kana uchitida tinogara pano- If you welcome us, we will stay here.* This shows that Gwenyambira is also a medium of interaction between the living and the dead. In this case, the audience has to be aware of the power that lies in Gwenyambira to overlap the land of the living and the land of the dead- music, and mbira playing then takes on a spirituality that other instruments of music do not have or has not been investigated. Flexing the same power of being a medium, Gwenyambira knows when the audience is aroused and what to say to confirm it. While Chiwoniso uses *Iiiiwee!*, Ambuya Beauler Dyoko uses *Maiweee!* In Shona, the word is an expression of regret, but it also is an expression of the height of pleasure. Again, such expressions punctuate the song when the audience is fully engaged. After that, Ambuya Beauler departs from the lament over a bad marriage and challenging family dynamics into idiophonic expressions that indicate that the atmosphere has been visited by superior spiritual beings, which Gwenyambira salutes as *Changamire*. There are repetitions of the ideophone *Tikinya that* describes motion, and this follows the salutation *Changamire*. One would be justified to assume that the motion being described is of the beings being saluted as *Changamire*.

## Chapter 19

## Conclusion

Nhemamusasa, is a traditional music that has various themes. Themes expressed in the two renditions of the song play an important role of expressing different episodes of the history of Shona people. The aspects of Shona life that constitute fundamental values of Shona traditions are expressed in different ways in the renditions that have been examined.

Conflict, whether it be military or in a domestic setting is a major destabilizing factor of human life. *Wakaringe zuva nhamo ichauya iwe, Kuroora roora ndaroora nguruve, Roverera museve*, are all expressions of different conflict situations that social commentators seek to make known. Conflict often hits hard on the innocent and unassuming- *wakaringe zuva nhamo ichauya iwe*. Conflict can destroy a person who is innocently watching the sun if it is violent. The weak in society bear the brunt of the impact of conflict,

The song and the history associated with it explain some of the confusion that existed in the church community of Zimbabwe, where some church institutions struggle to acknowledge the ability of black women to lead. There is a history behind such attitudes which is steeped in a history of deliberate disenfranchisement of indigenous women based on unfounded fears, stemming from the era of Mfecane that colonial settlers interpreted wrongly, thereby worsening the predicament of the standing of the Shona woman in society. Although that negative standing of the woman was initially associated with Shona women initially, it has spread to include women in general. Women of color in general struggle to shake off negative stereotypes on the African continent, and in the diaspora because there has not been enough done to invest in studying the core of who a woman of color is.

In the case of Nhemamusasa, a subregional problem of Mfecane caused a lot of changes among people in parts of the country that were occupied by Shona tribes. Later on colonial settlers who were ignorant of the experiences of Shona people prior to their coming worked through some missionaries to oppress Shona women even more. Shona women were a social group that needed to be liberated but even missionaries were heavy handed in their assessment of Shona women's standing, resulting in punitive policies that worsened the condition of an already weakened social group. The missionary church could have been a liberating force, but it did not extend the requisite compassion on Shona women. While this historical narrative still causes some churches to hold women in secondary status, it is never too late for those that hold the reins of power to enact laws that seek to reverse the centuries old system of relegating women to subservient roles in decision making both in church and government.

The major question our society can ask today is whether the Shona tradition is oppressive on its women or it was a colonial practice handed down to a society that received the subjugation of its women without questioning, and perpetuated it? Are the practices that we call Shona tradition, products that were handed down to the Shona people from generation to generation.? Nhemamusasa, exposes one issue that our society needs to revisit. It is to relegate some as well as improving other structures of leadership roles of men and women in politics and the church. It is not an issue of one gender oppressing another, but rather a system that distorted the existing traditional structures for mischievous reasons. Over the centuries, there has been no contemporary effort to question how we came to accept that women are not able leaders, and any role that they assume needs a male figure to supervise it openly or covertly.

## Sources

Ambuya playing **Nhemamusasa** in the garden, Copake, NY mbira

https://www.youtube.com/watch?v=X48CLpfmcyI

Chigwedere, Aeneas (1980) *From Mutapa to Rhodes* Macmillan

DES008, ( OCTOBER 2, 2012) *Nhemamusasa song* https://des008.wordpress.com/2012/10/02/nhemamusasa-song/

https://search.yahoo.com/search?fr=mcafee&type=E211US739G0&p=colorism&guccounter=1

https://en.wikipedia.org/wiki/Grammatical_tense

Mutswairo, S. M. (1980). *Feso*. Germany: Walter.

Mutsvairo, S. M. (1994) *Chaminuka prophet of Zimbabwe* Harper Collins

Reed, W. Lawrence (May 1, 2015) *Harriet Tubman: She never lost a passenger, Real Heroes* Foundation for Economic Education https://www.google.com/search?q=what+was+harriet+tubman+famous+for&oq=what+was+Harriet+Tubman+famous+for&aqs=chrome.0.0j0i22i30l5j0i390.9904j0j9&sourceid=chrome&ie=UTF-8

Thornton, Mae, Thornton, Willie. Wade in the Water, Sweet Honey in the Rock 1988 Lyrics © BMG Rights Management, Sony/ATV Music Publishing *LLChttps://www.lyrics.com/lyric/27341827/Sweet+Honey+in+the+Rock/Wade+in+the+Water*

Ambuya playing **Nhemamusasa** in the garden, Copake, NY mbira

https://video.search.yahoo.com/search/video;_ylt=AwrOsoVPdvxhkpw9BFL7w8QF;_ylu=c2VjA3NlYXJjaAR2dGlkAw--;_ylc=X1MDOTY3ODEzMDcEX3IDMgRhY3RuA2NsawRjc3JjcHZpZZAM4bTRyQXpFd0xqSXl6W

XRHWUMxNUtRcjZNall3TXdBQUFBQ0VRU25f
BGZyA3locy1wdHktYnJvd3Nlcl93YXZlYnJvd3Nlc
gRmcjIDc2EtZ3AEZ3ByaWQcEZWdVRVVGR
RWDZtZkllUjM3N3lyQQRuX3JzbHQDNjAEbl9z
dWdnAzEEb3JpZ2luA3ZpZGVvLnNlYXJjaC55Y
Whvby5jb20EcG9zAzAEcHFzdHIDBHBxc3RybA
MEcXN0cmwwDMjkEcXVlcnkDbmhlbWFtdXNhc2
ElMjBiZWF1bGVyJTIwZHlva28EdF9zdG1wAzE2
NDM5MzU1MDI-
?p=nhemamusasa+beauler+dyoko&ei=UTF-
8&fr2=p%3As%2Cv%3Av%2Cm%3Asa&fr=yhs-
pty-
browser_wavebrowser#id=3&vid=5d74b2f8c2044f
6aa1985ef1338d73cc&action=view

Chiweshe, Stella- Nhemamusasa, Kasahwa, Early singles, Glitter Beat

https://video.search.yahoo.com/search/video?p=st
ella+chiweshe+nhemamusasa&fr=yhs-pty-
browser_wavebrowser&fr2=p%3As%2Cv%3Av%2
Cm%3Asb%2Crgn%3Atop&ei=UTF-
8#id=1&vid=0b8d4a1e453ea66097c781e08b56ca83
&action=view

Maraire, Chiwoniso, Nhemamusasa, Ancient Voices, 1998 Lusafrica https://video.search.yahoo.com/search/video?p=stella+chiweshe+nhemamusasa&fr=yhs-pty-browser_wavebrowser&fr2=p%3As%2Cv%3Av%2Cm%3Asb%2Crgn%3Atop&ei=UTF-8#id=2&vid=582e7c30e8312b9880c4ffd66e1e37a5&action=view

Spiritual Lyrics: I Stood On The River Of Jordan
https://www.traditionalmusic.co.uk/negro-spirituals/i_stood_on_the_river_of_jordan.htm

Oregon State University - School of Writing, Literature and Film, What is Satire? A literary Guide for English Students and Teachers

https://video.search.yahoo.com/search/video?p=what+is+satire+in+literature&fr=yhs-pty-browser_wavebrowser&fr2=p%3As%2Cv%3Av%2Cm%3Asb%2Crgn%3Atop&ei=UTF-8#id=1&vid=78172c569fe875113d175366fd53f04d&action=view

Randye Jones, The Art of the Negro Spiritual

Research, lecture and performance projects on concert spirituals

http://artofthenegrospiritual.com/

Schmidt, Elizabeth (1992) *Peasants, Traders, & Wives: Shona Women in the History of Zimbabwe, 1870-1939 (Social History of Africa)* Heinemann

Slave Songbook: Origin of the Negro Spirituals, *Black History walks*

PBS documentary History Detectives Slave Songbook tracing the development of Negro Spirituals and cultural connections to Africa

https://video.search.yahoo.com/search/video;_ylt=AwrOsoV_qwJiFEQuZ6n7w8QF;_ylu=c2VjA3NlYXJjaAR2dGlkAw--;_ylc=X1MDOTY3ODEzMDcEX3IDMgRhY3RuA2NsawRjc3JjHZpZANiM1NrZFRFd0xqSXl6WXRHWUMxNUtRZldNall3TXdBQUFBQTlXNTdnbBGZyA3locy1wdHktYnJvd3Nlcl93YXZlYnJvd3Nlcg RmcjIDc2EtZ3AEZ3ByaWQQDZmJZOW5MVmhRbFMuMWpVUE1uemRWQQRuX3JzbHQDNjAEb9zdWdnAzAEb3JpZ2luA3ZpZGVvLnNlYXJjaC55YWhvby5jb20EcG9zAzAEcHFzdHIIDBHBxc3RybAMEcXN0cmwDMzMEcXVlcnkDaGlzdG9yeSUMG9uJTIwTmVncm8lMjBzcGlyaXR1YWxzBHRfc3RtcAMxNjQ0MzQyMjkz?p=history+on+Negro+spirituals&ei=UTF-8&fr2=p%3As%2Cv%3Av%3Am%3Asa&fr=yhs-pty-browser_wavebrowser#id=2&vid=0538ca219777ecb958fbbf0b6f3effa0&action=view

https://search.yahoo.com/yhs/search/?hspart=pty&hsimp=yhs-browser_wavebrowser&param2=0c9baf1b-7d79-4cee-b2d9-4ea7335b50db&param3=wav~US~appfocus1~&param4=d-cp12992494448-lp0-hh6-obgc-wav-vuentp%3Aon-igGpUiOAFECEtlpxeyRA-ab36-w64-brwsr-obx~UnknownDefault~what+is+a+syllable~B2D7D7656EB4E5153688637C8FBF7B49~Unknown&param1=20210825&p=what+is+a+syllable&type=A1-brwsr- ~2021-35~

www.ingramcontent.com/pod-product-compliance
Lightning Source LLC
Chambersburg PA
CBHW051426090426
42737CB00014B/2856